AF504084

WATERWISE

WATERWISE

GORDON FAIRLEY

William Luscombe Publisher Ltd
in association with
Mitchell Beazley Ltd

First published in Great Britain in 1974
by William Luscombe Publisher Ltd,
Artists House, Manette Street, London W1V 5LB

ISBN Hardback: 0 86002 002 9

ISBN Paperback: 0 86002 003 7

Filmset by Trade Spools, Frome
Printed by Alden & Mowbray Ltd. Oxford
Bound by the Pitman Press, Bath
Printed in Great Britain

Contents

Illustrations
Plates

Photographs Nos. 1–8, 11 and 13–15 reproduced by courtesy of Thames Television Ltd., and Nos. 9, 10 and 12 by courtesy of A. Greenway.

Line diagrams by Andrew Farmer

'I never was on the dull, tame shore,
But I loved the great sea more and more.'
Bryan Waller.

CIRCA A.D. 1800

'He that will not sail till all dangers are over,
must never put out to sea.'
Thos Fuller.

CIRCA A.D. 1732.

'And all I ask is a windy day, with the white clouds flying,
And the flung spray, and the blown spume,
And the seagulls crying.'
John Masefield.
(1878–1967)

By the time that I had finished writing this book, I was convinced that I had tried to pack too much into it. I hope that my friends are right in saying that I have managed to touch on the really important topics about which the beginner should, at least, be warned. I hope, also, that I have informed and encouraged many a beginner to begin!

It is a wise man who understands that he has never finished learning and an equally wise man who realizes that the contents of this book isn't all that there is to learn! The book is written directly along the lines of the series of television programmes which have been prepared with the assistance of many experts. The reader, or viewer, is assumed to be *any* member of the family. It is a book for the family. The crew must be able to tie a bowline, and the owner (Dad) must be able to choose the right equipment. The galley slave (Mum) must be able to take command of something more than the saucepans in an emergency and Junior, we hope, will become quite aware of the difference between a bed sheet and a jib sheet.

In my job at the Royal Yachting Association I have been in constant contact with people whose whole life has been, and is, connected with sailing and power-boating. I have learned from each of them something of what they know. Ocean racing skippers, dinghy sailors, coaches and instructors, cruising boat owners, canoeists, lifejacket experts, schoolmasters, editors of yachting papers, foreign sailors – the list is endless and I am sure that they would not all agree on every little detail. I would like to thank particularly John Rhodes, who asked me to help with the Thames Television series *Waterwise*; Bill Luscombe who thought this book worth publishing; Ian Sothcott, and the staff of Raven's Ait Sailing Centre at Surbiton; my colleagues at the R Y A for allowing me to reproduce some of their writings and methods of teaching, especially Bill Anderson, who offered much helpful, constructive criticism on the clarity of the text.

The Inland Waterways Association and the British Waterways

Board for allowing me to reproduce the excellent instructions on 'how to work locks without the assistance of the lock-keeper'; the Met. Office for their assistance in the section on weather; and last but not least the British Canoe Union officials and Tom Nisbet and Charles Currey for all their friendly help and guidance.

The lines from John Masefield's poem *Sea Fever* reproduced at the beginning of this book are quoted by kind permission of The Society of Authors as the literary representative of the Estate of John Masefield.

The list of enthusiasts is endless and, if I have forgotten to mention anybody, or forgotten to include essential information which you, the reader, might have found useful, the fault is mine, and I apologize in advance. I wish you safe and happy 'boating' in the craft of your choice.

Gordon Fairley
Petersfield,
Hants.

1. *Taking to the Water*

In pursuit of recreation man frequently attempts to emulate a great number of other creatures. By using our brains we have learnt to fly like the birds, we sometimes behave like mountain goats and, like ducks, many of us seem to be taking to the water. Some of us even emulate the lemming, famous for its periodical suicidal dashes into water.

This book is not for those who seek to copy the birds, but is concerned with the safety and well-being of all who choose boating as their particular form of recreation. It is also concerned to limit the number of human lemmings!

There is much to learn on specific subjects within the world of 'boating', and no *one* book can provide all the information which is needed. In fact, as has often been said, 'there is no teaching but experience'. This book therefore sets out to give broad-based general information, but always with the underlying principle of explaining where, how, in what and when the beginner on the water should start.

Those who already have some knowledge of the sport may not find the advice given here presented in the way in which they have been taught. However, there are, as the proverb says, 'more ways than one of killing a cat' – and similarly there are many ways of ensuring that those enjoying a sport stay alive.

The glossary of nautical terms at the end of the book (see page 148) is not intended to baffle the newcomer with science. The vocabulary used in the text will not, generally, be that of the seasoned seafarer, although all the words which he *does* use for specific ropes and similar gear will, of course, be used to ensure that there is no confusion on board, when the reader eventually gets afloat.

Your motives and your motive power

What drives you on the water may be your arms, a sail or an engine. There are many sorts of craft and the first thing a beginner 13 must decide upon is what kind of boating he personally wishes to undertake.

When you begin, don't be too ambitious. Sailing looks easy, and motor-boating even easier, but both appear deceptively simple when done by an expert. So first, you really MUST learn.

You *can* learn by just getting in a boat and trying it out. However, this is certainly not the way to be recommended, especially if you wish to use the wide blue sea to its best advantage.

If you want to learn

Many organizations, with their addresses, are listed at the back of this book, and in my opinion, learning to sail or drive a power-boat is best achieved by attending a teaching establishment.

The Royal Yachting Association runs many schemes of proficiency and can help to find adequate tuition for you and your family. The Sports Council also runs courses for nearly every sport, and sailing is no exception. Students at school can often learn to sail, even in school time, and their particular sailing organization is the National School Sailing Association. Those who wish to canoe should contact the British Canoe Union, or the Scottish Canoe Union. In addition, more and more local authorities are starting up Outdoor Activities Centres to teach canoeing, sailing and other skills. So it isn't difficult to get taught!

Other sources of information are the advertisements in the yachting magazines, while advice from the local sailing, motor-boating, canoeing or water ski clubs will be given willingly.

But, PLEASE, don't just buy a boat, push it in the water, loaded with your precious family, and float or drown according to your good or bad luck.

Learning to drive a power-boat

Small runabouts with big outboard engines are fun! There are, however, many rules, especially the Rules of the Road (a special sort of Highway Code for those at sea) so it pays to attend a course at an evening institute, even if the course calls itself *Navigation*, which may frighten you off a bit. Don't let it.

If you want to use some of the many miles of rivers and canals, your knowledge of 'seamanship' does not need to be too profound, but there are still many things to learn, so that you won't endanger yourself and others. The Inland Waterways Association produce a very good guide, with lots of information for people like you.

Before you actually buy your boat, it may well be worth hiring a cruiser for an inland waterways holiday. Try not to roll up to take delivery from the hire fleet owner, and then ask him to teach you to 'drive' her. He will, but it is hardly fair to expect the hire fee to stretch that far.

Buying your first boat

The purchase of a boat is not, as I have explained, the first thing to do. If you buy a dinghy before you have learnt to sail it, the entire family gets wet, tired and cold before they can appreciate the pleasures. I have seen a family wading home, towing the damn thing, because nobody could sail it. So do learn first.

Choosing your boat

There are broadly eight varieties of craft for those involved in boating, fishing or sub-aqua activities.

The smallest variety is the *dinghy*: an open boat of up to about 16 ft in length. Taking a sailing dinghy as a specific example, you should consider the following points before signing the cheque for its purchase.

1. Can you trail it behind your car, or carry it on the roof?
2. Do you want to . . .?
3. Can you and your wife lift the thing?
4. Do you have time to look after a wooden dinghy, or would a glass fibre one be better?
5. Is it water-worthy (seaworthy)? The vast majority of sailing dinghies are well equipped with buoyancy. They will FLOAT upside down – and you *will*, sometime, go upside down! An ordinary rowing boat will not float if it gets full of water.

Most, not all, dinghies have 'built-in' buoyancy (using the seats and fore-deck as sealed air boxes). Some have sausage-shaped air bags which, for the pottering type, are more likely to get punctured.

6. Where will you use it – and will you want to join the local club?

7. Does your local club have *that* sort of boat? If you roll up and say 'Here I am with my new XYZ dinghy; I want to join in the club activities' and you get a rude answer indicating that the club does not use your sort of dinghy, you are likely to be slightly put out. One of the Royal Yachting Association booklets,

by the way, tells you what clubs sail, in the way of classes of dinghy.

These then are *some* of the questions which you must consider before pulling out your pen and cheque book.

For boats to be used with outboards, items 1 to 5 are worth thinking about. An outboard is a heavy thing. And don't forget that you can't get out and walk if your outboard stops! It is worth ensuring that you buy one in tip-top condition, and *keep it like that ever afterwards.*

Buying a 'runabout'

There are some special considerations for these boats. There *is* a maximum size and weight of engine. After a certain point, whatever power you have on the back end, the speed will increase relatively slightly. Don't get carried away by the gleaming monsters on display. They are heavy to carry about and tend to cause the bow of your boat to lift dangerously.

Boats for fishing

These come in many sizes, but should always have adequate shelter for the area in which you intend to fish. Sea boats really should have a covered-in front end (half-deck) and, for longer excursions, cooking and toilet facilities. Anglers need bags of elbow room and safety equipment, as well as anchors (plural . . . in case you lose one), warm and waterproof clothing and lifejackets. It is a long way to the shore sometimes. The coastguard have a very good pamphlet called *How Safe Is Your Craft?* which is a great aid to deciding what to take on board. I shall be dealing in more detail with equipment later (under *Seamanship*).

River boats

If you want to use the canals, remember that the *maximum* width of boat is 6 ft 10 in.

For river cruising enthusiasts, an afternoon's 'recce' will give you a good idea of the craft and equipment which other people find satisfactory. On the Thames, for example, motorized craft are of endless variety but, if you never intend to go to sea, or even in estuarial waters, you can swop a bit of 'seaworthiness' for higher sides, shallower draught (depth below water) and large windows (which would get smashed at sea). Without being rude, river craft *can* afford to be a little more like caravans if there are no waves or strong winds.

Sea-going boats

There are motor cruisers, sailing cruisers and what are known as 50/50's. The latter have a larger engine than the average sailing cruiser, and a smaller sail area. They are 'belt and braces, best of both worlds' craft and generally very seaworthy.

Motor cruisers really should have two engines and these must be absolutely independent of each other – from fuel tank to exhaust. If one 'dies', you can limp home on the other. If there *is* only one engine, or a joint fuel system to two engines – well, you try rowing a high-sided motor cruiser, or rigging up some sort of sail out of nothing! If you have only one engine, at least take a small outboard (and fix a proper mounting for it).

Statistics show that the largest number of recreational craft in some sort of trouble are those with engine defects and no alternative means of propulsion – other than the R N L I boat, the coastguard or a friendly helicopter winch-man!

Plate 1. Even sailors have to learn to paddle!

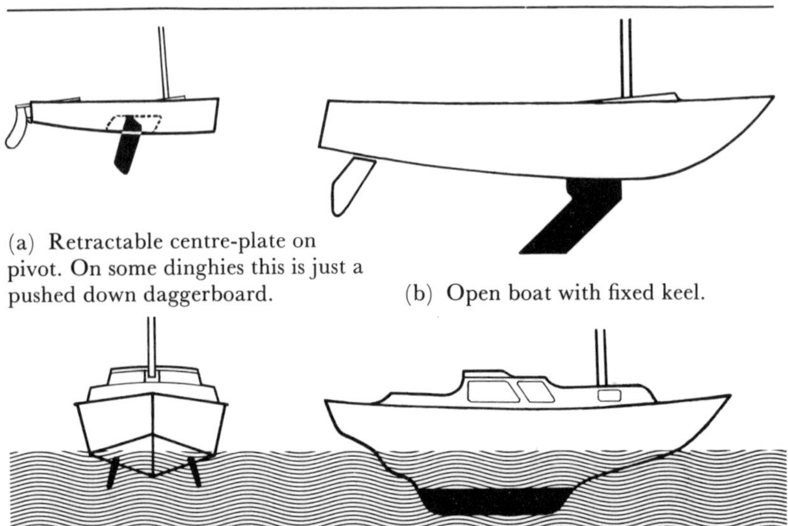

(a) Retractable centre-plate on pivot. On some dinghies this is just a pushed down daggerboard.

(b) Open boat with fixed keel.

(c) Twin keel cruiser. Such keels run either side of the boat's bottom to enable the boat to negotiate shallower water than a single-keeled boat, and to 'sit on the ground' without falling over.

(d) Fixed keel cruiser. There are hundreds of different designs but all are fixed and faired in with heavy ballast to counterbalance the wind pressure on sails.

Fig. 1. Types of underwater shape.

Sailing cruisers

These craft are primarily driven by sails (with a small auxiliary engine for 'close quarters' work or when the wind drops). They have various underwater shapes which are illustrated in Fig. 1.

Boats for diving

There are many small boats which can be used for this sport. Some different shapes of boat are illustrated in Fig. 2.

Boats for water ski-ing

Water ski-ing is not just a question of buying skis, a tow-line and what you believe to be a suitable boat. The sport is a great deal more difficult than it looks. The British Water Ski Federation will put you in touch with a federated club. Go and talk to them, bearing in mind that, because of the high speeds required, and

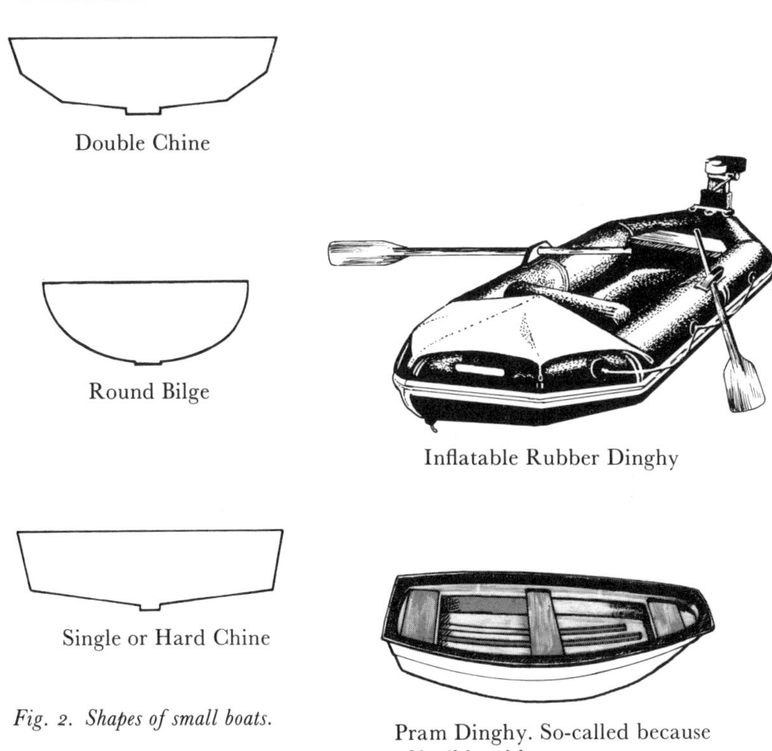

Fig. 2. Shapes of small boats.

the possible risk to bathers, there are many places where water ski-ing just 'ain't allowed'. Furthermore, there are often limits to the number of boats allowed to use a designated area.

Canoes

The three basic types of decked-in canoe (with the general name 'kayak') are illustrated in Plate 2. The 'skirt' worn by the canoeist is illustrated at Fig. 3, serving its proper function. The 'slalom' is a banana-shaped boat; the touring canoe, in the middle, will carry a fair amount of equipment; and the racing canoe is long and lean, with a rudder, and is the most difficult to use. The degree of balance required, in comparison with the other two, is very marked. Each has a special paddle and all are double-ended. They either have foam plastic buoyancy or air bags securely fixed into their hulls.

Plate 2. Three types of kayak. Note the spray deck already attached
to the canoeist

*Fig. 3. The deck arrangement on a kayak
canoe.* The canoeist wears a soft spray
deck which is elasticated. As soon as
he is in the canoe, he fits this over
the lips of the cockpit, thereby
making his canoe virtually
watertight. When he wishes to leave
the canoe, he pulls the strap in front
of him which immediately releases
the spray deck from the canoe.

In all kayaks you adjust the foot-rest so that you can relax your
legs to escape in the event of capsize. In the racing canoe, the
points of contact are really only the feet and your backside. In the
others, you can brace your knees against the sides of the canoe
which also helps your balance.

All the 'kayaks' are decked-in but the majority of the Canadian
canoes are not. In these canoes, the paddler kneels and uses a
single-bladed paddle. These, also, are designed for either racing,
slalom or touring.

Safety in canoes

The British Canoe Union suggests that if you cannot swim, you
should not use a canoe. I heartily endorse this statement, having

Plate 3. The first stages of learning include safety drills

watched canoe capsize drill. You *must* learn this drill. It is clearly well worth while to seek out the nearest Canoe Union coach whose address will be available at the Local Education offices.

The BCU Director of Coaching will help with expert advice on all training matters, and the General Secretary, who will also give you advice about where you can and cannot canoe, may be contacted at 70, Brompton Road, London, SW3 1DT.

In Appendix 3 you will find more detail about canoeing proficiency.

Canoes at sea

I need hardly say that canoes in a seaway are vulnerable! Canoeists in Wellington boots are mental and canoeists who don't take all the necessary gear are liable to be lethal . . . to themselves! I have set out an equipment list for small boats in Chapter 5. I suggest

Plate 4. When using a lock, share it with other craft whenever possible, and so save water

that intending canoeists read it, because it also applies to canoes at sea. In your waterproof bag you should carry flares, whistle, torch and an exposure bag. You should even think about a compass. You are no different to the other mariners except that it is a little difficult for you to use the international distress signals listed in Chapter 5. The beach rescue organizations and the Corps of Canoe Lifeguards will understand a raised hand or paddle, as will most other experienced and intelligent seafarers. I don't, however, recommend that you stand up in your canoe and slowly raise and lower your arms!

Inland waterways

22   There are many thousands of boats on our inland waters and the

membership of the Inland Waterways Association constantly expands. The IWA produce several publications, but the *Inland Waterways Guide* published by *Boat World* Publications contains many useful hints and tips. Perhaps information about the use of locks which you have to work yourself is the most vital.

Working the locks

There are, of course, waterways where the locks are attended by staff, such as on the Rivers Trent, Severn and Thames, but these are the exception, rather than the rule.

Speed limits (4 m.p.h. on canals and 6 m.p.h. on rivers) are imposed to avoid damage to the banks of the waterway, or to moored craft and they should be respected. Craft meeting each other should pass each other left side to left side. That means DRIVE ON THE RIGHT. In most countries this doesn't feel odd because they drive their cars on the right. To us, it is a bit unusual but it *is* the international rule. The 'tooting', which commercial craft do, should be known, and perhaps used by pleasure craft as necessary. One 'toot' means 'I am turning my ship to starboard (right)'. Two 'toots' means 'I am turning to port'. Three 'toots' means 'My engines are going astern' (although the vessel may still be moving forward, he has started to reverse her or, in other words, he is 'putting on the brakes'). When you hear a vessel giving FIVE short 'toots' it means 'I don't think you are taking sufficient action to avert collision', or 'What the devil ARE you doing – and have you seen me at all?' Especially in narrow channels you, in your small boat, are duty-bound not to impede larger craft which can only navigate in the deep channel. The other thing to watch for is a heavily loaded commercial boat which may have to keep to the deep channel and therefore navigate on the outside bend of a river. He will probably choose the side upon which he wishes to pass. YOU GIVE WAY; he's working – and must not go aground.

Also, please consider carefully where you are going to moor up. Don't 'park' on a blind bend – you wouldn't on the roads. Don't park under a bridge. Try to choose a straight stretch where everybody can see you, and be able to slow down to pass you.

Before I set out the Inland Waterways Association instructions for working locks I would like to explain one or two technical terms. Water can be let into a lock by two methods. There are usually 'sliding doors' in the locks themselves. If you wind these up, the resulting square hole lets the water into the lock. Alternatively, there may be similar equipment on the bank outside the lock gates. These 'sliding doors' work in exactly the same way, but the water is let into a pipeline which runs round the gates and into the lock. In either case the machinery you are operating is called a 'paddle'. Here is a diagram (Fig. 4) of a possible paddle system. The fact is that you won't find ground paddles on all locks, by any means. In the diagram 'P' equals paddle and 'GP' equals ground paddle.

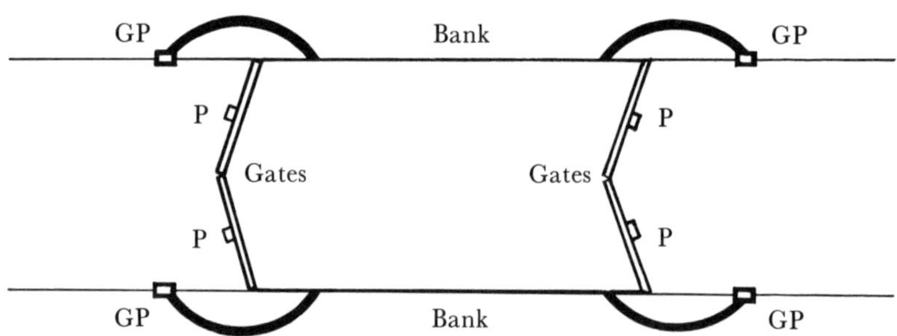

Fig. 4. Plan view of a lock 'paddle' system.

Now to tell you how to work the locks (this section reproduced by kind permission of the Inland Waterways Association and the British Waterways Board):

Except on such rivers as the Thames, Severn and Trent, and on busy commercial waterways, the navigator works the locks for himself. Hirers of craft should be instructed on the operation of locks before they set off from the hire base.

The golden rule is 'never waste water'. Study the lock working instructions on pages 26 and 27. The lock drill should be followed systematically and the following points observed:

a. To conserve water ensure that all paddles are wound down when leaving the lock. If the gates are leaking, as a result of damage or bad fitting, close all gates before leaving. Close all gates at the top lock of a flight and the last lock before a long pound.

b. If a lock is closed 'against' you on arrival do not empty or fill it if a boat is approaching it from the opposite direction. Let the approaching boat lock through first.

c. Where side-ponds are provided on canal locks, use them. If you are not familiar with the use of side-ponds, follow the instructions which are usually displayed on the notice board beside them.

d. NEVER SLAM GATES SHUT OR DROP PADDLES OUT OF CONTROL – This may cause damage to them or injury to you. Close the gates by hand and WIND THE PADDLES DOWN. Do not open lock gates with the bows of your boat.

e. If two pleasure craft approach a lock together they should work through together (if they will both fit in). This saves water.

f. Draw the ground paddles first where both ground and gate paddles are provided on canal locks. Draw the gate paddles only when the paddle entrances are under water. On river locks where no ground paddles are provided, open the gate paddles slowly. Compliance with these instructions will prevent excessive turbulence in the lock and avoid damage to your boat.

g. Keep your boat clear of the cill situated underneath the top gates when locking downhill.

h. When locking uphill, boats should be secured to the bollards provided at the lockside but do not secure the boat when locking downhill or it will be left suspended as the water falls – give the mooring lines to a member of your crew on the lockside to hold when locking downhill.

i. DO NOT LEAVE WINDLASSES ON THE SLUICE MECHANISMS when the lock is filling. If the mechanism slips the windlass will fly off, possibly causing PERSONAL INJURY or its loss in the lock.

All this may sound complicated and daunting but it soon becomes second nature. Please see full instructions, with diagram, on pages 26 and 27.

Trailing your boat, and insurance required

Before you have the towing hitch put on to your car, investigate the insurance situation and the law on towing trailers.

Generally, your motor-car insurance will cover you, after you have informed your motor insurers, for the act of trailing the boat, even if it is detached, by mistake, from your car and goes careering into somebody else's garden. However, as soon as you *deliberately* detach the boat from the car in order to pop it into the water, your motor-car insurance ceases to be operative. That broadly is the situation. You must therefore take out insurance with a yacht insurer for the next set of risks. These can be of two major kinds. First, damage to the boat itself and its bits and pieces, theft, etc. The second kind is against 'third party liability' for property or

A Going uphill * lock empty

Top gates will be shut and paddles (P) and (Q) closed.
A1 Enter lock.

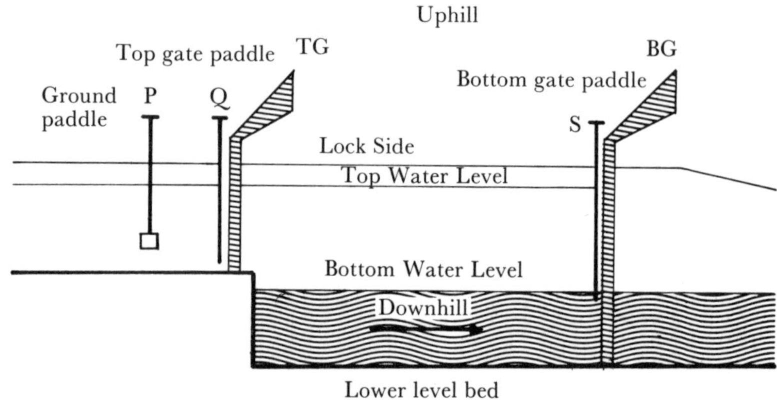

Fig. 5. Side plan of a lock 'paddle' system.

A2 Close bottom gates (BG). *See bottom gate paddles (S) are closed.*
A3 Open ground paddle (P).
A4 Open top gate paddle (Q) when submerged.
A5 When lock is full – open top gates (TG).
A6 Leave lock. *Close top gates, close all top paddles.*

personal damage. This is a kind of hidden risk in the sport and you must be insured against it.

It is not possible to set down the conditions of insurance because they vary from policy to policy. I have set out, in full, the most recent rules about trailing boats. These have not been in force for all that length of time and even some experienced sailors may still be driving about as 'outlaws'.

You should also be warned that there are some very general laws about carting 'dangerous loads' on the roads. The law says that it is an offence to take anything which MIGHT be a danger to you or others on to the roads. You will see that this is, indeed, very wide-ranging. If you are towing an outboard-engined boat, always take off the engine, if possible, and stow it in the bottom

B   Going uphill * lock full

B1   Close top gates (TG). *See top gate paddle (Q) and ground paddle (P) are closed.*
B2   Open bottom gate paddles (S).
B3   When lock is empty open bottom gates (BG). Proceed as in A1–6 above.

C   Going downhill * lock full

When locking downhill, moor vessel in lock clear of top gate cill.
C1   Enter lock. Bottom gates will be shut and paddles (S) closed.
C2   Close top gates (TG). *See top gate paddle (Q) and ground paddle (P) are closed.*
C3   Open bottom gate paddles (S).
C4   When lock is empty, open bottom gates (BG).
C5   Leave lock. *Close all bottom paddles (S) and bottom gates.*

D   Going downhill * lock empty

D1   Close bottom gates (BG). *See bottom gate paddles (S) are closed.*
D2   Open ground paddle (P).
D3   Open top gate paddle (Q) when submerged.
D4   When lock is full open top gates (TG) and proceed as in C1–5 above.

---

of the boat. If you can't get the engine off, either because it is too heavy or is bolted on, then see that it is well 'padded' and protected. Outboard engines project rather a long way and can cause a nasty accident if you are in a 'shunt'.

Generally speaking, you can assume that the manufacturer of a trailer has complied with the law. He is likely to go rapidly out of business if he has not. You, on the other hand, must make sure for yourself. If you are towing any kind of a boat, you must have the trafficators and brake lights hitched up to your car. For this purpose there are a number of people manufacturing a complete kit, all mounted on a board with room for your trailer number plate as well. The lights can all be fixed through to the car by the addition of a plug and socket.

There are special rules about the amount of 'overhang' you may have, so see that the mast, if you have one, doesn't stick out over the stern.

The most recent set of regulations permit higher speeds provided you conform with the requirements. The speed limit for private vehicles (not above 30 cwt. unladen weight) towing boat trailers is increased to 50 m.p.h. except where a lower general speed limit applies. However, the ratio between the weight of the trailer and the towing vehicle is the all-important factor and, even if you don't meet the requirements so that you can go at 50 m.p.h., you should, for your own safety *and* that of others, not tow a heavy trailer with too light a towing vehicle.

The conditions for travelling at 50 m.p.h. (where there is no lower general speed limit) are:

1. the relevant weight of the trailer must not, if fitted with brakes, exceed the kerbside weight of the towing vehicle or, if unbraked, exceed 60 per cent of that weight;

2. the towing vehicle must be clearly marked with its kerbside weight either inside the vehicle or externally on the left or nearside;

3. the trailer, if it is either a caravan or a trailer carrying fixed equipment, must be clearly marked with its maximum gross weight on the external nearside;

4. a plate with the number '50' must be fixed on the trailer in a vertical position facing squarely to the rear.

Combinations not complying with these conditions are restricted to 40 m.p.h. on all-purpose roads and, if the trailer is of the single axle or two close-coupled axles type and the towing vehicle is 30 cwt. unladen or below, to 40 m.p.h. on motorways.

The 'kerbside weight' is the weight of the vehicle without driver or passengers or any load other than fuel, water and normal tools, but including the weight of any towing bracket with which the vehicle is normally equipped.

The 'maximum gross weight' is the weight which the trailer is designed or adapted not to exceed when in normal use and travelling laden on a road.

Weights may be expressed in either imperial or metric units but the same units must be employed for both the towing vehicle and the trailer. If metric units are used the weights must be shown in kilograms.

A 'close-coupled trailer' is one in which the wheels are not steerable and the distance between the centres of the front and rear wheels does not exceed 33 in.

The '50' plate may be circular or elliptical and if the latter, so placed that the long axis is horizontal. It must be coloured black with the number 50 in white, silver or light grey. The *minimum* dimensions are:

> Circular plate: 4 in. diameter
> Elliptical plate: 3 in. height, $4\frac{1}{4}$ in. width
> Each digit of the number: $1\frac{3}{4}$ in. height, $1\frac{1}{4}$ in. width
> Width of every part of figures: $\frac{5}{16}$ in.
> Space between figures: $\frac{1}{4}$ in.

If the figures are raised then they must not project from the surface of the plate by more than $\frac{3}{16}$ in.

Clearly it is an 'offence' to display this 50 plate on a trailer if you do not comply with the regulations. So, if you tow different boats about, you must cover up the plate if you are not conforming with the regulations. These regulations do not apply to vehicles registered abroad which are visiting this country for not more than twelve months. This is a point to remember when *you* are going abroad. See to it that, if you are required to comply with the laws in foreign countries, you know what they are.

Whilst you can trail canoes, it is more usual to load them on to a well-padded roof rack, using rope (not elastic cord) because the windage is terrific. If you have a very small car, make sure that the rear 'overhang' is within the law.

Opportunity knocks!

You do not have to own a boat in order to enjoy sailing. You can easily hire a river cruiser, and the inland waterways stretch for many hundreds of miles. You can find many sailing clubs on gravel pits and reservoirs (and many more on rivers) and you can certainly find sailing in the schools and youth groups round the country.

There are many grades of British Canoe Union Proficiency Schemes, and the Royal Yachting Association runs similar Schemes for day sailing boats, motor launches and power-boats, coastal craft and the yachtmaster's examinations in conjunction with the Department of Trade and Industry.

Because these schemes are at present the only truly national 29 schemes, a brief explanation of the basic idea behind the schemes might be useful here. I have already said that there are many places to learn, but what is the basic information which you should have?

RYA proficiency

The syllabus for the RYA Elementary Certificate for Dayboat Sailors perhaps sets this out as clearly as anything I can write. The full syllabus is set out in Appendix 3. This and the more advanced certificates right up to coach grade, are contained in a log book, in which you can keep a record of your own 'seatime'. Another log book can be kept if you are one of the enthusiasts for sail training ships, in which there are many splendid opportunities of really tasting the salt water under expert tuition in some excellent craft, the like of which you could never have dreamed of sailing in ten or fifteen years ago. Please read the detailed syllabus of the RYA Elementary Certificate. It looks daunting, but with proper teaching, can be 'hoisted in' during one week of hard work. It is worth it to ensure the safety of your whole family. Clearly it is designed for the sailing boat owner but there are many hints and tips for the canoeist, for anglers and for the owner of a fast runabout boat.

Canoe training

In Appendix 3 you will find the full syllabus of the BCU Sea Proficiency test for a kayak conoeist. You will note that the test suggests that you should go to sea with a competent leader. *Of course*, the Elementary and Inland Proficiency tests are a good deal less difficult.

2. Boat-wise and Weather-wise

The vocabulary of the boat

A study of Figs. 6 and 7 will help you to become familiar with the names given to the principal parts of a boat. Of course, only a small part of the sailor's vocabulary is included in the diagrams,

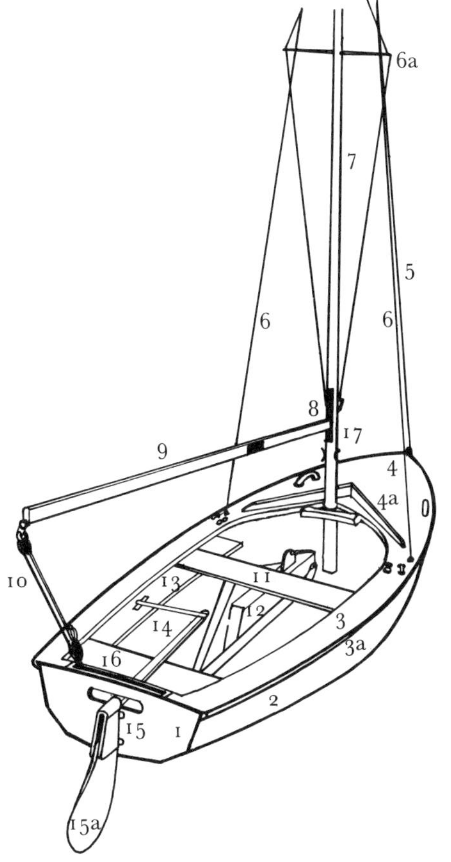

1. Transom
2. Hull
3. Side deck
3a. Rubbing strake
4. Foredeck
4a. Washboard (to stop water!)
5. Forestay from bow to masthead
6. Shrouds
6a. Spreaders or crosstrees
7. Mast
8. Gooseneck (swivel fitting, joining boom and mast)
9. Boom
10. Mainsheet and 'Blocks'
11. Thwart
12. Centreboard case
13. Built-in buoyancy
14. Tiller and tiller extension
15. Rudder stock
15a. Rudder blade
16. After deck
17. Cleats

Fig. 6. Principal parts of a boat

1. Burgee (if square, racing flag)
2. Mast
3. Forestay
4. Jib hanks
5. Jib tack strop
6. Clew of jib
7. Boom
8. Battens in batten pockets
9. Bow (or stem)
10. Centreboard
11. Stern
12. Mainsheet
13. Jibsheet
14. Jibsheet lead

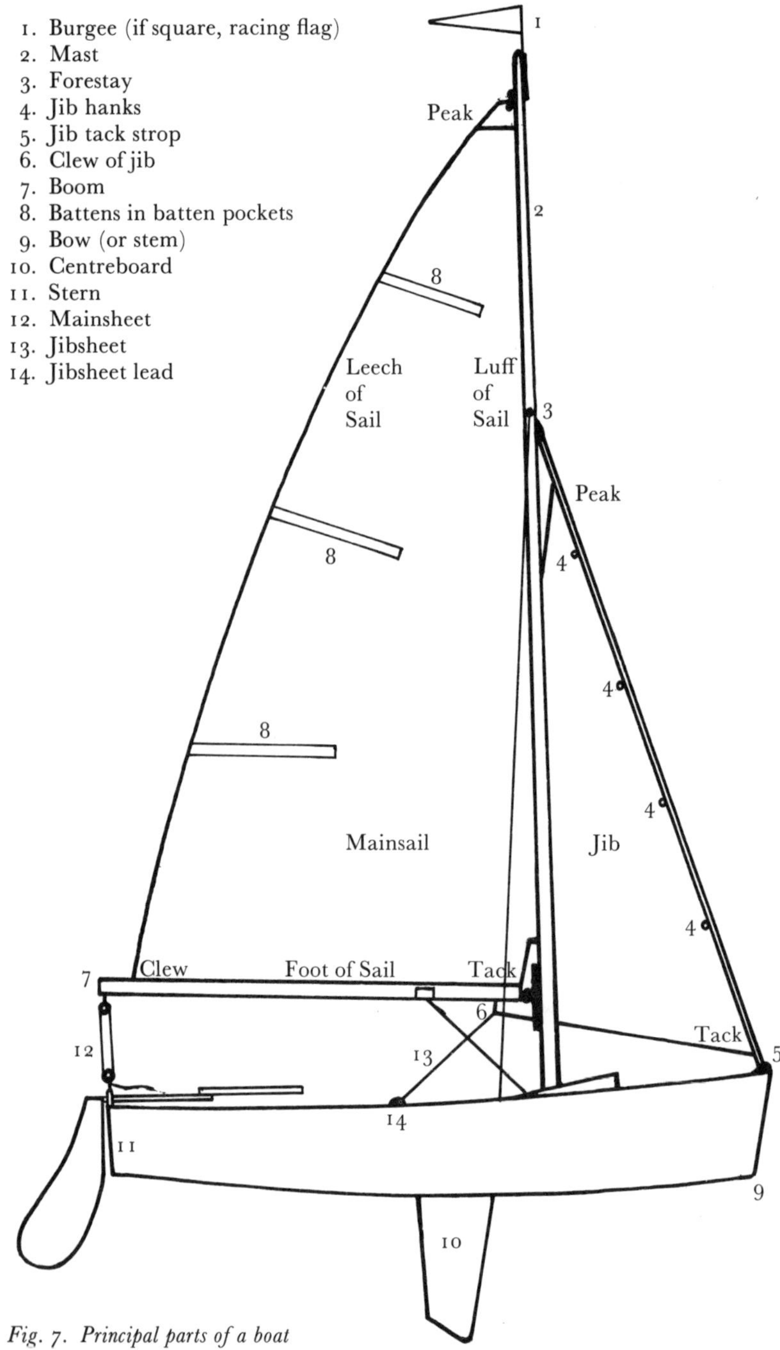

    Fig. 7. Principal parts of a boat

but you will find many other terms, with an adequate description, in the glossary of terms at the end of this book (page 148).

I would just refer to larger vessels for one moment, since I shall be using technical words connected with them later on in the book. All around the cruising craft are posts with wires joining them. These are known as stanchions and guard rails. At the bow, there is a construction to stop one falling overboard, aptly called a pulpit, and at the stern a similar construction, which for obvious reasons is often known as a *pushpit*!

Parts of the boat

Two other words, which are almost impossible to illustrate, must also be explained before we go much further. The ropes which pull the sails up the mast or forestay are called 'halyards'. This term is a corruption from the old days when you needed to 'haul yards' (the spars upon which square sails were hung).

The ropes which you use to control the tightness of the sails (letting them out or tightening them in) are called 'sheets'. Hence 'sheeting in' your sails means making them tighter, and 'easing sheets' means exactly what it says! The shrouds, forestay and, in some cases, backstay are all called 'standing rigging'. The 'blocks' (No. 10 in Fig. 6) are pulley wheels round which the mainsheet travels.

It is difficult to illustrate every type of 'cleat' to which you will be attaching and making fast your various halyards, etc., but the most common looks like this:

Fig. 8. A common cleat.

In some cases, it will be clear that you can jam the rope by a last turn. In other cases it will be necessary to secure the rope by finishing off with a hitch like this:

Fig. 9. A hitch on a cleat.

However, *sheets* should never be hitched. There are many occasions when you will need to let them go in a rush.

Weather, wind and water

Nothing indicates the action of the wind and tide better than watching a beach ball disappear when it has accidentally been kicked into the sea. The tide and the wind can be extremely useful to those who understand them but, for those who push off from the beach without the three W's in their mind, there can be trouble. I am talking about WATER, WIND AND WEATHER...

Water: the moving sea

The tides rise and fall TWICE every twenty-four hours, and they are caused by the gravitational pull of the sun and the moon. The tides are either very high and then very low (these are called 'Springs', or 'Spring Tides' and have nothing to do with the seasons) or they are of much less range, not so high nor so low. These are called 'Neaps' or 'Neap Tides'. Whilst they are rising and falling they cause tidal streams and it is these that concern you, in your small boat on the sea.

In one area on the South Coast, as an example, the tidal stream reaches $8\frac{1}{2}$ m.p.h. so that if you sit on a plank, or in a boat, and do nothing, you will float gracefully along at that speed, quite rapidly disappearing from view! ADD the strength of your engine (or sails) and away you go even faster. Since the tide turns roughly every six hours it will be a long time before it starts to float you back to point A, so you will virtually be going 'uphill' when you turn round at the end of two hours jolly boating.

The wind

As we all know, the wind is variable and can be very strong. If it is blowing *against* the tide it can make the sea very rough, and it can *also* mean that you may have trouble returning to your point of departure. A gust in the garden and a squall at sea are about as different as a bow and arrow and a field gun and shell!

I have set out briefly the reasons why you should know which way the tide is going, ebbing or flowing, and where you are in relation to it. Later in the book, we will see why it may take you longer than you think to get home. You can sail in a straight line with the wind behind you, but not with it against you. You have to 'zig-zag' and the distance to sail is therefore at least double.

The weather

The scene is a lovely summer day – a day for shirt-sleeves and ice-cream. Yet two hours later, cold and wet, you are wondering whether it is January rather than August. The lesson is clear: if setting out in a boat, even if you don't intend going far, take many more clothes than you apparently need, and strip them off whilst it is hot. And also take a lifejacket. If weather, wind and water combine to turn your boat over (heaven forbid!), *do not leave it while it is still floating. You cannot beat the tide by swimming. Distances are deceptive and a boat is easier for rescuers to see than a number of small heads dispersed over an area.*

The weather map

The lines on the weather map are known as isobars, and are plotted by drawing a line through all places of equal atmospheric pressure. It is the pressures that matter to you. From them, originate all the changes of weather. The weather map as illustrated in Fig. 10, is a sort of contour map of pressure distribution.

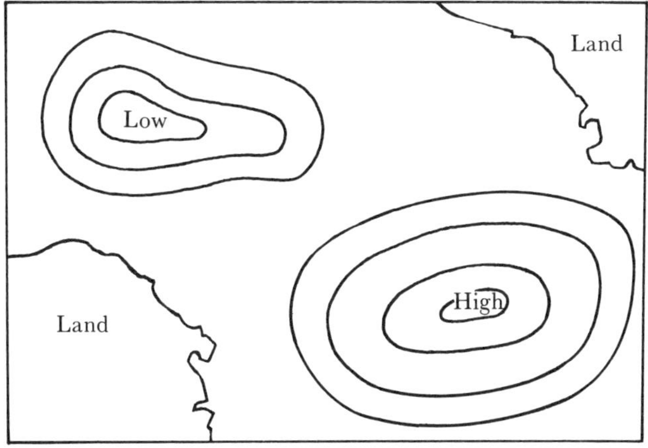

Fig. 10. A weather map.

Areas of high pressure

These provide most people's idea of good weather. Nothing much happens. In summer, the weather is usually fine, with hazy sun and not much wind, although there will be sea breezes. It is usually calm in the morning and evening though fog can form, especially in the autumn. High pressure does not change rapidly so that these areas of high pressure (known as anticyclones) give settled spells of fine weather. It is safe to assume that the day will remain reasonable and that strong winds are unlikely until the 'high' starts moving away.

Areas of low pressure

These are aptly named 'depressions'. There will be wind, cloud, rain and showers. The weather is likely to change quite rapidly. Special attention should be paid to local forecasts and an eye kept on clouds and wind. A *deep* depression, which is announced over the radio, will be one where the pressure is unusually low in the centre, and *you* can expect gales if the depression is in your area.

Changes of pressure

In a small boat, whether under sail or power, you are going to be affected by the wind. If you get wet, this does not particularly matter, but it is the *wind* that is important. Differences of pressure cause winds. Winds at the surface of the earth blow roughly along the isobars of the weather map, being deflected slightly towards the centre of a depression. They always blow the same way round a depression (due to the rotation of the earth) so that if you stand with your back to the wind you can be sure that the low pressure will be to your left. If high cirrus clouds (very high, white or golden) are moving from your left, you can expect the weather to deteriorate. If high cloud is moving from the right, there is likely to be an improvement, and if the same clouds are moving in the same direction as the surface wind, there will be little change.

Fronts

Figure 11 shows the formation of fronts in a depression and Fig. 12 a cross-section through a frontal depression. If you see the high cirrus cloud on your left, a 'warm' front is approaching, and you can expect a depression with strong winds at the surface

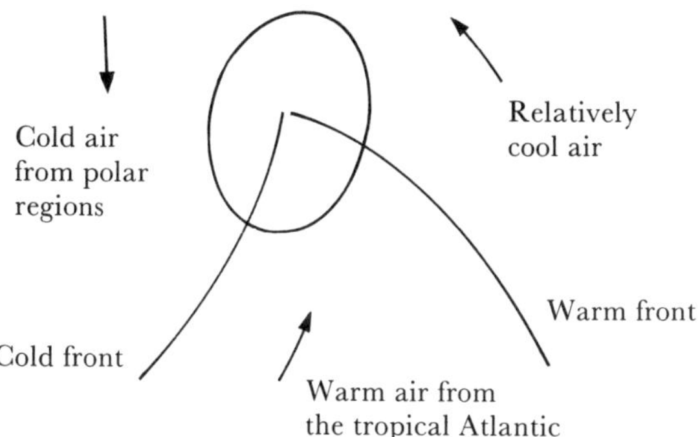

Fig. 11.

(which will affect you) later on. Watch the barometer which will start to fall. The surface wind will probably come from the south. This warm front will *eventually* arrive at the surface during the rain period. The wind will probably be stronger as the front passes and will then tend to veer westwards and decrease in strength.

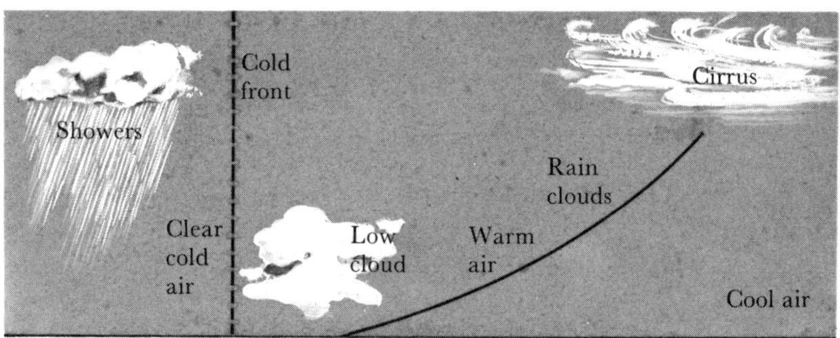

Fig. 12.

Cold fronts arrive concealed by the low cloud of the warm sector. It will rain harder and then clear. Blue skies and clear air with excellent visibility will move in from the west, and you will heave a sigh of relief that the weather has cheered up. In fact, you can *then* expect more vigorous weather. The wind will be stronger than at any other time during the progress of the depression. Squally showers, with attendant gusts, could upset you and your little boat.

Summer weather away from depressions

In ordinary summer weather there is a definite daily sequence of cloud, possible showers, sea breezes, etc.

A typical day might be: *Morning* – sunny, little or no cloud, calm. *Later* – still calm, small cumulus clouds begin to form. (These clouds are formed by warm air rising from newly heated land. As air rises it expands and cools, and at a certain height it will have cooled to the temperature of the 'dew point'. Here the water vapour condenses and becomes visible as a cloud.) These small puffy clouds, called 'fair weather cumulus', should be familiar to everyone. If the atmosphere is meteorologically stable, these will be the only clouds all day. The cloud bases will get higher as the day goes on but the clouds will remain small. In these conditions sea breezes will only be slight.

The formation of sea breezes usually starts about eleven in the morning. Warm air rising over heated land – the air forming the cumulus clouds – is replaced by air moving in from the water which will have stayed at a more steady temperature. The sea breeze effect is most marked on a definite straight coastline of sea one side, land the other, but can occur anywhere, even on small lakes. Sea breezes will build up to a maximum by early afternoon and can give a good vigorous sailing breeze near the coast. Often, on the landward edge, much bigger clouds can be formed, which can be seen before the breeze actually starts. The sea breeze effect stops, as the land begins to cool in the late afternoon, and the sea breeze will die out in the early evening. A sea breeze can modify winds resulting from weather systems and its effect should be looked for locally by all sailors.

Showers

The air is unstable. Clouds will start to tower up higher as the day goes on. Although the air is cooling as it rises, it is remaining warmer than surrounding air and thus keeps rising.

Big towering cumulus clouds soon give showers. This is because, when water droplet clouds rise high enough they are cooled to below freezing point. Eventually ice crystals start to form.

Most of the top of the cloud becomes ice crystals. This is easily seen from the ground as the top of the cloud suddenly goes all fuzzy, losing its cauliflower-like appearance. Ice crystals grow until they are too heavy and then fall, melting on the way, to give raindrops. These kinds of showers will reach maximum activity in the afternoon and die away to give a fine clear evening.

Thunderstorms

These are huge shower clouds. The rising air is so vigorous that the winds near a thunderstorm will blow in towards the cloud, at the earth's surface. A thunderstorm thus usually seems to be approaching against the wind. As the storm arrives there can be very severe gusts from any direction. There will be heavy rain or hail and the wind direction can change completely (and suddenly) due to strong downdraughts within the storm. Avoid such storms if possible and watch from the shore. If caught out in one, reduce sail and keep awake for wind changes. Thunderstorms can usually be seen (and often heard) sometime in advance so there is plenty of time to avoid them.

Effect of showers on an airstream wind

Forces within a shower cloud are similar to those within a depression. Thus, winds in front and to the left will be increased, whilst winds at the back and to the right will be decreased (Fig. 13). The usual sequence is strong wind in front of the shower with a squall as the rain arrives. There will be rain while the shower is overhead and then the wind and rain die away as the cloud moves off. The wind increases again soon, and may increase further as another shower approaches. The general impression on a day of many showers is that the strongest winds are under the blue sky patches.

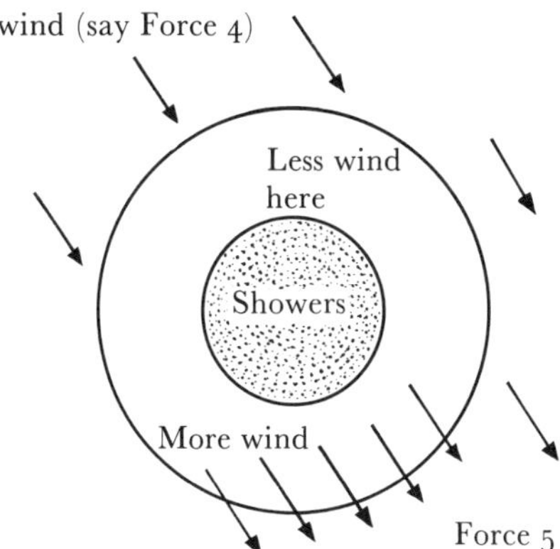

Fig. 13. Forces within a shower cloud.

Forecasts

General forecasts are made at midday one day, for the whole of   39 the next day so, they cannot be all that precise. Add to this the difficulty of describing weather in everyday language and peoples' lack of observation, and it all becomes pretty vague. Shipping forecasts are much more technical, and up-to-date, but summer weather is very drastically modified by the land. When in doubt, contact the local weather station (number in phone book). They are usually very helpful and will have the latest chart in front of them. *In British weather there is no such thing as a sudden change.* By observing the clouds and wind you always get advance warning of weather changes.

Relationship between appearance of water surface and wind

Wind strength can be seen from the surface of the water. The scale varies according to the size of the water but the appearance of the waves is still the same.

Force 0   Calm. Smooth and flat.
Force 1   Just enough wind to mark the water.
Force 2   Small waves are formed in a definite pattern.
Force 3   Small waves; a few of the waves become unstable and small 'white horses' are visible when looking towards the wind direction.
Force 4   Larger waves, 'white horses' widespread when looking towards the wind direction.
Force 5   Big regular waves with large breaking tops, the 'white horses' are now visible for some way when looking downwind, looking upwind the sea looks very rough.
Force 6   Very rough. Waves big and irregular. Looking upwind the white horses seem to be in long lines. Looking downwind, there are streaks of foam showing from the breaking wavetops which are all visible. The water near at hand will have a streaky appearance from foam.

Above Force 6 is purely academic for small boat sailors; they can invent suitable descriptions in the bar!

More about forecasts

My wife always tells me (since she listens to the radio to keep her company when ironing or doing the other dreary chores round the house) that the Shipping Forecasts are a closed book to her. Well, that's all right. Who cares what the weather is like when doing the ironing? What is disturbing, however, is the thought that a large number of people who should understand them, AND listen to them, do not do so.

There are an increasing number of forecasts put out on the radio. Apart from these, the local harbour master, fishermen, and even the local R A F station will give you a very reasonable idea of what to expect and will tell you over the telephone.

Self-help is just as good. The main shipping forecasts are put out on Radio 2 on 1500 metres at the following times:

> 0030 hrs
> 0630 hrs
> 1355 hrs (1155 on Sunday)
> 1755 hrs

The words 'wind', 'force', 'millibar' and 'visibility' have been omitted from weather bulletins broadcast by the BBC. This is to enable the forecast to be given in a clearer and more concise form in the time available.

You will hear things like 'five miles, 1008 falling slowly'. This sort of statement does not mean that they are observing a shooting star numbered 1008 approaching earth! It indicates that the visibility at that place is five miles and that the barometric pressure is 1008 millibars and is falling slowly – which means that the weather is likely to worsen.

Because of the importance, to you, of the weather forecasts I now reproduce, by kind permission of the Meteorological Office, much of the detail contained in the Meteorological Leaflet No. 3: *Weather Bulletins and Gale Warnings for Shipping*. This pamphlet is updated every year but the latest, at the time of going to press, reads as follows:

Contents of broadcasts

The broadcasts will consist of the following items:
  (i) A statement of the gale warnings in force at the time of issue of the forecasts.
  (ii) A general synopsis giving the situation in so far as it affects the area within the next 24 hours, with information as to expected changes within that period.
  (iii) Forecasts for the next 24 hours for each coastal sea area, giving wind speed and direction, weather and visibility. The areas will be given in a fixed order. When appropriate, contiguous sea areas may be grouped together (see Fig. 15).

41

Fig. 14. Stations whose 2200 reports are included in the Radio 4 Inshore Waters Shipping Forecast.

(iv) The latest reports from a selection of the following stations will be broadcast in this order, the number of stations depending on the time available: Wick, Bell Rock Lighthouse, *Dowsing*, *Galloper* and *Varne* light-vessels, Royal Sovereign Light-tower, Portland Bill, Scilly/St Mary's, Valentia, Ronaldsway, Prestwick and Tiree. The elements given will be wind direction (compass points) and speed (Beaufort force), present weather (including 'past hour' weather), visibility and, if available, sea-level pressure and tendency in qualitative terms.

Forecasts for coastal sea areas are normally broadcast in the following order:
Viking, Forties, Cromarty, Forth, Tyne, Dogger, Fisher, German Bight, Humber, Thames, Dover, Wight, Portland, Plymouth, Biscay, Finisterre, Sole, Lundy, Fastnet, Irish Sea, Shannon, Rockall, Malin, Hebrides, Bailey, Fair Isle, Faeroes, South-east Iceland.

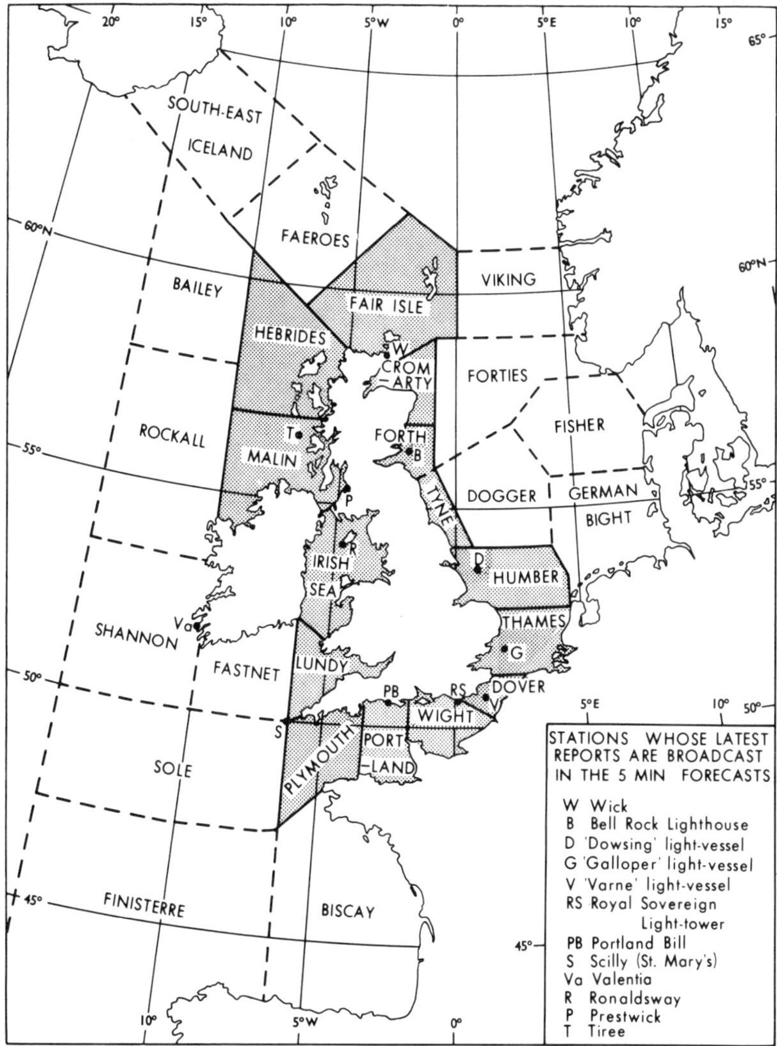

Fig. 15. Boundaries of sea areas as used
in BBC and Post Office weather forecasts.

BBC Radio 4

Forecasts for inshore waters (up to 12 miles offshore) of England and Wales 'until 1800 tomorrow' are broadcast at the end of the English and Welsh Radio 4 programmes. The forecast of wind, weather and visibility is followed by the 2200 reports of wind direction (compass points) and speed (Beaufort force), present weather, visibility and, if available, sea-level pressure and tendency in qualitative terms from the following stations: Acklington (near Newcastle), Gorleston (near Great Yarmouth), Manston (near Ramsgate), Portland Bill, Scilly/St Mary's, Mumbles (near Swansea), Aberporth (Cardigan Bay) and Ronaldsway (Isle of Man).

At the end of the Northern Ireland Radio 4 programme a similar forecast for Northern Ireland inshore waters is given with 2200 reports from Kilkeel (County Down), Killough (County Down), Malin Head, Machrihanish (Kintyre), Ronaldsway (Isle of Man), Valley (near Holyhead) and Orlock Head (near Bangor, Northern Ireland).

The forecast for Scottish inshore waters is given towards the end of the Scottish Radio 4 programme with the 2200 reports from the following stations: Machrihanish (Kintyre), Tiree, Stornoway, Wick, Aberdeen (Dyce) and Leuchars.

Details of precise times and frequencies are published in the *Radio Times*.

Gale warnings

Gale warnings are issued when mean winds of at least force 8 or gusts reaching 43 knots are expected. The term 'severe gale' implies mean winds of at least force 9 or gusts reaching 52 knots. The term 'storm' implies a mean wind of at least force 10, gusts reaching at least 60 knots. The term 'imminent' implies within 6 hours of the time of issue; 'soon' implies between 6 and 12 hours: 'later' implies more than 12 hours.

Visual gale warnings

Gale warnings are sent immediately to those places where visual signals (cones or lights) are displayed. The Admiralty publishes details in the appropriate Sailing Directions.

The display of a visual gale warning signal indicates that a gale is expected within 12 hours, or is already in progress, in the coastal sea area adjacent to the station displaying the signal. Thus a visual signal at Hartland would indicate a gale warning in operation for the sea area Lundy.

The signal will be lowered when the wind is below gale force, if a renewal of gale-force winds is not expected within 6 hours. Thus, the signal is left flying during a temporary abatement of a gale if a renewal is expected.

The areas to which the visual gale warnings apply are shown shaded in the maps in Fig. 15.

The North Cone, a cone point upwards (by night, a triangle of lights apex up), is hoisted for gales from any point north of the east–west line. The South Cone, a cone point downwards (by night, a triangle of lights apex down) is hoisted for gales from any point south of the east–west line. When the direction of the gale is expected to change from the northern side to the southern side of the east–west line, the North Cone is lowered and the South Cone hoisted. Conversely, when the direction of the gale is expected to change from the southern to the northern side of the east–west line, the cone is changed accordingly.

Information given by these cone signals is to be regarded only as supplementary to the more detailed weather bulletins for shipping which are regularly broadcast from BBC and Post Office transmitters.

Weather bulletins for shipping

The words 'wind', 'force', 'millibar' and 'visibility' are omitted from weather bulletins issued in plain language from Post Office and Irish Coastal Stations. This is to enable the forecast to be given in a clearer and more concise form in the time available. Forecasts cover the period 24 hours from the time of issue.

Coastal areas

Weather forecasts, giving wind speed and direction, weather and visibility, are broadcast on w/t and r/t from coastal radio stations appropriate to the area to which the forecast refers.

Reports of present weather

People requiring reports of actual weather conditions prevailing at specified places around the coast of the British Isles may obtain such reports by telephone from any of the stations in the following list. (Such reports only apply to present weather in the immediate locality of each station and do not include forecasts or information concerning other areas.)

The various types of stations are distinguished as follows:

Meteorological Office	Met.O.
Coastguard Stations	C.G.
Lighthouses	L.H.
Signal Station	S.S.
Harbour Master's Office	H.M.O.

Name of station	Telephone number at time of going to press	Type of station
Scilly/St Mary's	Scillonia 651	C.G.
Tol-Pedn-Penwith (Gwennap Head)	Sennen 219	C.G.
Lizard	Lizard 444	C.G.
Mount Batten (Plymouth)	Plymouth 42534	Met.O.
Prawle	Chivelstone 259	C.G.
Beer	Seaton 14	C.G.
Portland Bill	Portland 3100	C.G.
Needles	Freshwater 2265	C.G.
Calshot	Fawley 484	S.S.
St Catherine's Point	Niton 284	L.H.
Thorney Island	Emsworth 2355	Met.O.
Shoreham-by-Sea	Shoreham-by-Sea 2226	C.G.
Newhaven	Newhaven 131	L.H.
Eastbourne	Eastbourne 20634	C.G.
Fairlight (Hastings)	Pett 3171	C.G.
Dungeness	Lydd 236	L.H.
Folkestone	Folkestone 54230	C.G.
Dover Strait (St Margaret's)	St Margaret's Bay 2515	C.G.
Manston	Manston 351, Ext. 220	Met.O.
Sheerness	Sheerness 3025	S.S.
Shoeburyness	Shoeburyness 2271	Met.O.
Thames (Walton-on-Naze)	Frinton-on-Sea 5518	C.G.
Aldeburgh	Aldeburgh 2779	C.G.
Gorleston	Gt Yarmouth 63444	C.G.
Cromer	Cromer 2507	C.G.
Spurn Point	Spurn Point 283	C.G.
Flamborough Head	Flamborough 203	C.G.
Whitby	Whitby 2107	C.G.
Middlesbrough	Easton Grange 2541	H.M.O.
Tynemouth	North Shields 72691	C.G.
Seahouses	Seahouses 274	C.G.
St Abbs Head	Coldingham 287	L.H.
Usan (Montrose)	Montrose 1	C.G.
Fraserburgh	Fraserburgh 3374	C.G.
Lossiemouth	Lossiemouth 2121	Met.O.
Kinloss (Moray Firth)	Forres 2161, Ext. 16	Met.O.
Tarbatness (Moray Firth)	Portmahomack 210	L.H.
Wick	Wick 2215	Met.O.
Lerwick	Lerwick 239	Met.O.

Kirkwall (Orkneys)	Kirkwall 2421	Met.O.
Cape Wrath	Scourie 267	L.H.
Stornoway	Stornoway 2256 (Night: 2282)	Met.O.
Rudh Re (Ross and Cromarty)	Gairloch 2481	L.H.
Benbecula (Hebrides)	Benbecula 351	Met.O.
Ardnamurchan (Argyll)	Kilchoan 210	L.H.
Tiree	Scarinish 41	Met.O.
Rhuvaal (Islay)	Port Askaig 202	L.H.
Kildonan (Isle of Arran)	Kildonan 211	C.G.
Ardrossan	Ardrossan 3972	H.M.O.
Prestwick (Firth of Clyde)	Prestwick 78475	Met.O.
Corsewall Point	Kirkcolm 220	L.H.
Portpatrick	Portpatrick 209	C.G.
Mull of Galloway	Drummore 211	L.H.
Carlisle	Carlisle 23422, Ext. 440	Met.O.
St Bee's Head	Whitehaven 2635	L.H.
Point of Ayre	Kirkandreas 238	L.H.
Ronaldsway (Isle of Man)	Castletown 3311 (Night: 3313)	Met.O.
Ballycastle	Ballycastle 226	C.G.
Bangor (County Down)	Groomsport 284	C.G.
Killough	Ardglass 203	C.G.
Kilkeel	Kilkeel 232	C.G.
Fleetwood	Fleetwood 3780	C.G.
Blackpool	Blackpool 43061 (Night: 43063)	Met.O.
Formby	Formby 72903	C.G.
Rhyl	Rhyl 3284	C.G.
Valley (Anglesey)	Holyhead 2288	Met.O.
Porthdynllaen (Caernarvon Bay)	Nevin 204	C.G.
Aberporth (Cardigan Bay)	Aberporth 205/208	Met.O.
Milford Haven	Milford Haven 2343	H.M.O.
Tenby (Monkston Point)	Saundersfoot 2722	C.G.
Mumbles	Swansea 66534	C.G.
Ilfracombe	Ilfracombe 2117	C.G.
Hartland	Hartland 235	C.G.

3. Sail-wise and Knot-wise

The theory of sail

Under this rather pompous title let me tell you a few of the interesting facts which your sailing instructor will be trying to get over to you during the few days which you will probably share with him and a lot of other students.

A wing on edge

You depend upon your senses and upon the elements to get the best out of a sailing boat. Many is the man who is reputed to 'sail by the seat of his pants'. In fact he is using sight, sound, touch and even hearing as he senses the power and direction of the wind. He depends on the elements of wind and water and prays that he may *never* encounter the element of fire at sea.

It is important for the beginner to understand HOW a sailing boat is driven by the wind. As one instructor puts it, 'Here comes another gust of FUEL; FUEL coming over your left shoulder, feel it coming. Here it is. MAKE USE OF IT!'

Most people know that an aeroplane obtains 'lift' from its wings. The action of the air *over* and under the wing tends to lift the plane off the ground. In the old days of small piston engines the wing area of an aeroplane had to be large (jets, of course, are more like a shell than like a bird or kite).

A sailing boat's sail is like a wing on edge. The action of the wind 'through' the sail is shown in Fig. 16. The wind passing round the back of the sail provides 'lift' and the resistance of the hull and keel to the water stops the boat blowing sideways. The combination of this resistance and the wind force means that, when the boat is being sailed as close to the wind direction as it will go without 'stalling', it is going as fast as ever it will. As one student put it, 'I am a bit vague as to whether one is being sucked along or pushed along. Whichever it is, I certainly made her go today.'

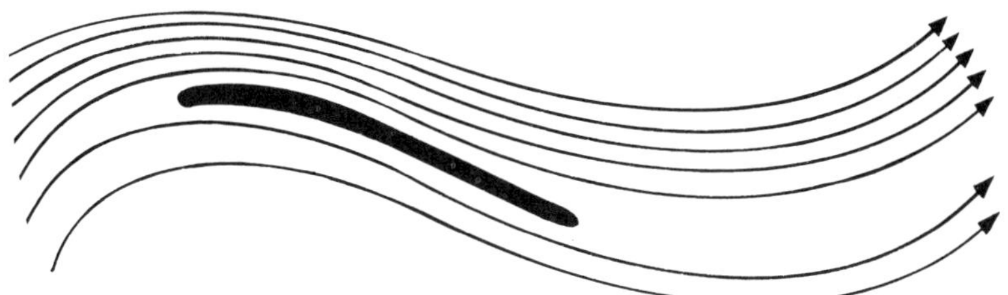

Fig. 16. Action of the wind 'through' the sail. Your sail is both pushing and pulling you. The centreboard of the boat and hull provide resistance and the combined effect is to push the boat forward through the water.

Points of sailing

Boat A in Fig. 17 is close-hauled. Now let's see what happens as the boat is turned slightly more away from the direction of the wind (Boat B). It needs less resistance under the water (so the 'keel', usually a liftable centre-plate in a dinghy, can be lifted halfway up). The sails are let out halfway and the boat stands up better. In fact, for a beginner, it is a very happy situation to be in. He can sail comfortably back and forth, getting the 'feel' of the boat.

Finally, let's look at Boat C. The boat has been turned to run away from the wind ('running before') and the sails are really acting exactly like an umbrella, and who has not experienced the wind under an umbrella? In this attitude, the boat is not being pushed sideways at all, so the 'drag-resister' (centre-plate) can virtually be raised right up.

I hope that it is clear from Fig. 17 (Boat C) that the forward sail (the jib) has ceased, in the boat on the left, to have any use-effect. It is completely blanketed by the larger mainsail. The *really experienced* (and the amateur in calm water) can fill the jib with wind by setting it on the opposite side to the mainsail and steering a very direct course *dead* downwind. Do not try it until you are reasonably skilled, because you may gybe (pronounced 'jibe') by mistake, and, unless controlled, this is a dicey manoeuvre.

It is necessary to explain gybing at some point, and since I have just warned you about it, this seems a good place to do so. As your boat goes downwind, you *could* turn it a bit too far to the right (starboard). As you do this, you will see from Fig. 18 that the stern of the boat passes through the wind. The wind will then push on the *front* side of your sail, and the unsuspecting will

49

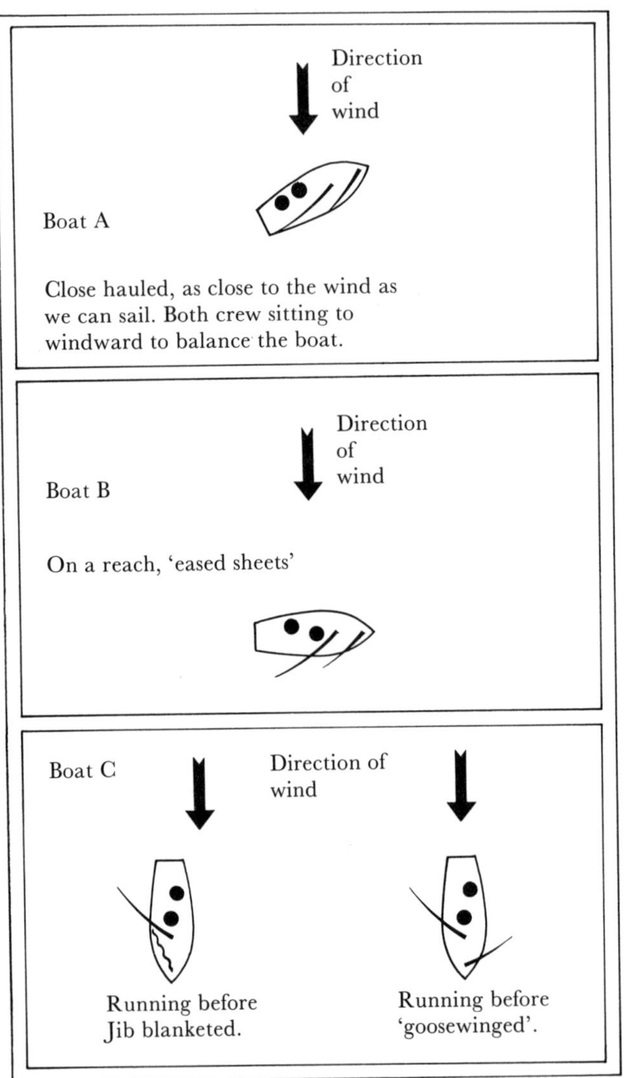

Fig. 17. Points of sailing.

get a crack on the head from the boom as it whisks SUDDENLY over to the other side of the boat. That's gybing.

Alternatively the *wind*, rather than the boat, could change direction (and quite frequently does) and that change of direction would produce exactly the same effect. That's gybing too, only it is even more likely to make you feel uncomfortable because you did not do it on purpose.

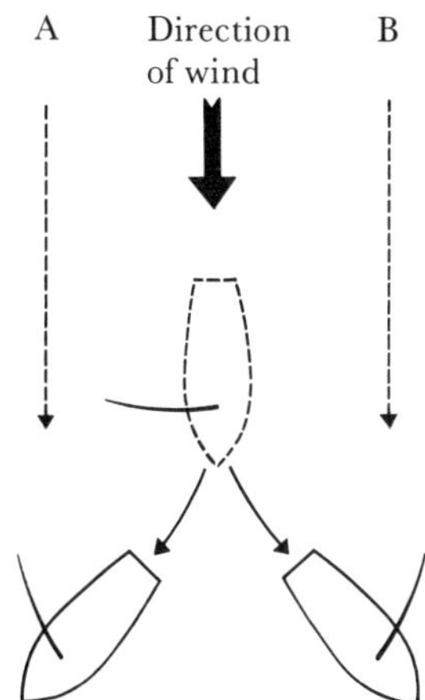

Fig. 18. Wind A (or wind B!) gets round the back of your sail – and, wham-bang, over she goes to the other side of the boat, before you even have time to shout 'gybe-oh!'

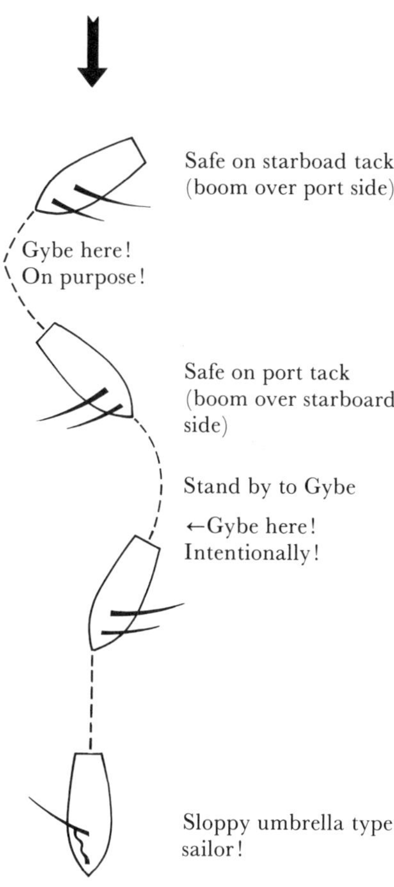

Fig. 19. Safety down wind.

I hope you can now see why I emphasise the words *really experienced* when talking about putting the jib on the opposite side to the mainsail and 'goosewinging' dead downwind. It is danger-ous to sail absolutely dead downwind and in fact also happens to be a rotten use of your FUEL. It is much safer to sail a slightly zig-zag course *to ensure that the wind, even if it changes direction slightly, is* definitely *on one side of your boat or the other* (see Fig. 19).

Turn again to Fig. 17 and let's see what the technical terms are for the different points of sailing.

Boat A is 'beating', 'hard on the wind', or 'close-hauled' (so-called, because the ropes controlling the sails are hauled in close).   51

The helmsman of Boat B has 'eased his sheets' and is sailing across the wind direction ('reaching').

Boat C is 'running before'.

All this explanation is necessary, and I hope not too complicated, to explain how to use your FUEL to the best advantage.

Now let's discuss what may already have become clear to you. If, as in Fig. 20, the wind is blowing DEAD from the direction in which you wish to go, you will not be able to sail directly there because the wind cannot blow on your sails at all. You will soon find how close you can go to the actual direction of the wind without 'stalling'. The only way you can get there is to zig-zag or TACK across the wind.

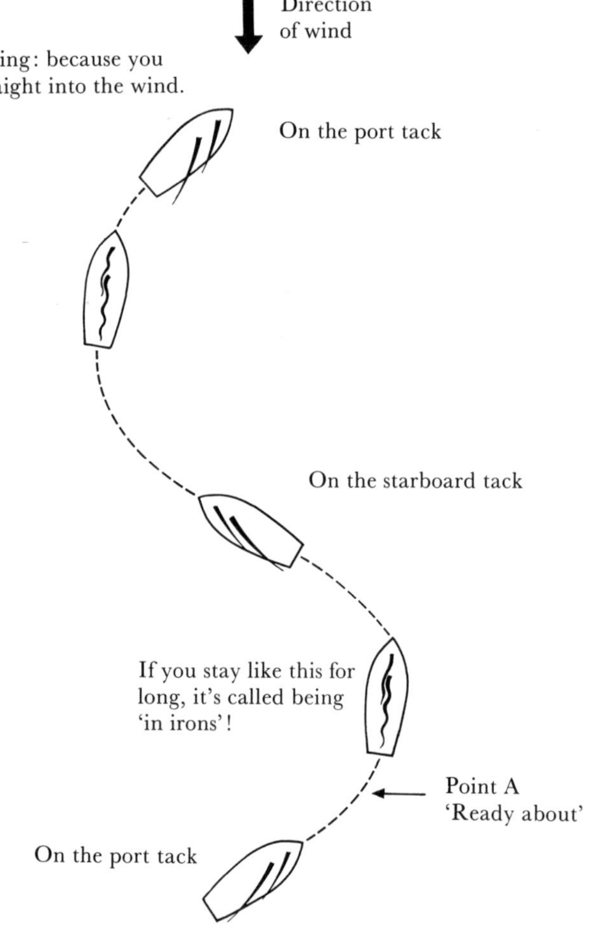

Fig. 20. Tacking: because you cannot go straight into the wind.

Tacking is easy. You are sitting with your back to the wind, balancing your boat. You ALWAYS sit up on the windy (windward) side holding the tiller in one hand and the mainsheet in the other. Your mainsheet hand should always be the FRONT hand. When you wish to turn at Point A (Fig. 20) you alert your crew by saying 'Ready about'.

When you are both ready, you say 'Lee-oh' and push the tiller firmly away from you. This brings the boat's head through the wind and you both move quietly and efficiently over to the other side, ready to balance it against the force of the wind. As YOU cross over, you will find it quite natural to change hands so that you hold the tiller with the hand nearest the stern and the mainsheet with the front hand.

The crew lets go of his tightened sheet just after you have said 'lee-oh' and all sails will shift over as the boat goes through the wind. As the boat straightens up so the crew 'sheets in' his sail on the other tack. All as simple as A B C, as you can see from Fig. 20.

Making fast

I remember once seeing an old lady painting a picture of what she called 'the beautiful yachts'. She was clearly a great artist, but no seaman. All the yachts in her picture were attached to the quay-side by a neat selection of ropes all tied in *bows*!

There are in fact several hundred knots but it is only necessary for the average pleasure craft owner to know a few. A 'Granny' knot is, of course, too awful to contemplate because it will not hold, and will not come undone when wet. It should therefore never be used in a boat.

Every seaman's knot has a special use, all are easy to untie and yet will remain tied until Doomsday.

Knots

The Reef Knot. This is used for tying together two ropes OF EQUAL SIZE when there is tension on both ends. It tends to slip if the ropes are of unequal diameter (these should be tied with a sheet bend). When you have finally tied a reef knot you will see that if you tug it in a particular direction it will 'spill' and slide undone.

Use it for 'tying up parcels' like the reef in a mainsail or round the mainsail when you have lowered it.

Lay the RIGHT hand end OVER the LEFT (like the start of a bow on your shoe), then LEFT OVER RIGHT. The finished knot has the ends on the same side, is flat and neat (see Fig. 21), unlike the Granny knot. So, RIGHT OVER LEFT, LEFT OVER RIGHT. Got it?

Fig. 21. The reef knot.

The Half Hitch. This is the beginning of many knots. Pass the rope round a piece of wood (try a chair back) and then pass the end through itself. Add a second half hitch in the same direction and it is pretty safe for hitching a line to a ring or post (Fig. 22).

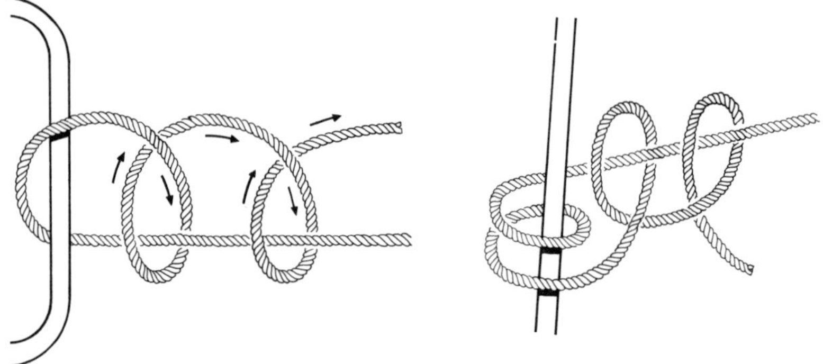

Fig. 22.. A couple of half hitches – *both* must go in the same direction.

Fig. 23. A round turn and two half hitches.

Turn the rope round the ring or post TWICE before doing your hitch and you have made, almost without thinking, a **Round Turn and Two Half Hitches** which should hold your dinghy even more securely, or a fender to the guard rail (Fig. 23).

Then we have the **Fisherman's Bend** which I have not illustrated, because it is just a ROUND TURN AND TWO HALF HITCHES with the FIRST half hitch actually passing through the round turn.

The Clove Hitch can be made up on either a spar or guard rail or used by making a couple of 'opposite' loops and slipping them over the end of a post (Fig. 24). It is also useful for tying the burgee halyard as illustrated in Fig. 25.

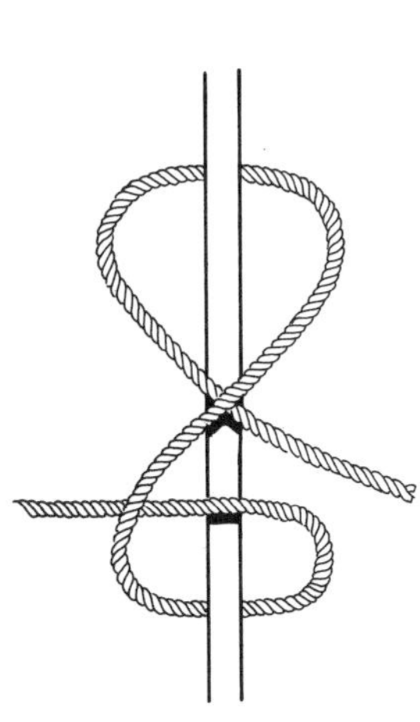

Fig. 24. Clove hitch slipped over a post.

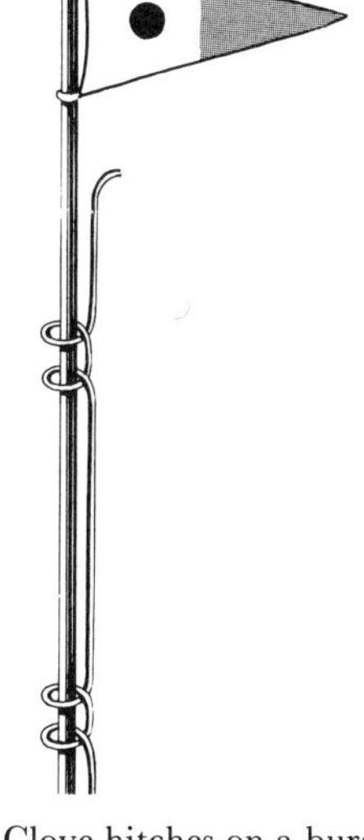

Fig. 25. Clove hitches on a burgee halyard which is an endless rope for putting the burgee at the masthead (where it should be *upright*).

Because there are a number of uses for a **Rolling Hitch** or **Stopper Hitch** when the strain is expected to be parallel, or nearly parallel to the axis, I illustrate the two 'phases' of tying this particular knot (Fig. 26). It always seems to be needed in a hurry and a specific case is referred to later in this book. Having tied the hitch, it can be made more secure by finishing up with a half hitch.

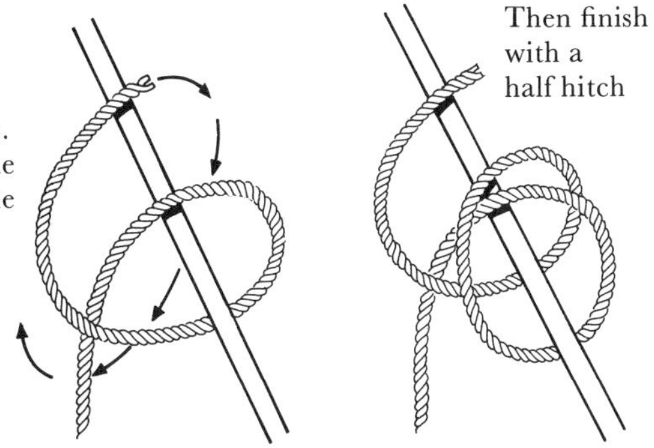

Fig. 26. *Left:* rolling hitch, phase 1.
Right: rolling hitch, phase 2. You must make sure that the second turn is jammed inside the first.

Then finish with a half hitch

The Bowline. This is my favourite, multi-purpose, knot, never impossible to untie, once learned never forgotten and nobody can criticize you when the dinghy has floated away because, in fact, it WON'T! As you can see from the picture, the completed knot forms a fixed loop in the end of a rope. You can make fast to a ring, post, bollard or cleat; tie it when the rope will be immersed by the tide; tie it round yourself if you have to be hauled up somewhere (and you won't crush your chest). It should be used to tie a sheet to your jib in larger boats and it can be used for tying two short ropes together to make, for example, a longer warp to reach the shore. If you can tie the bowline without thinking, then you can do almost anything on a boat. Incidentally you pronounce it to rhyme with 'roll-in'.

To tie the knot see Fig. 27:

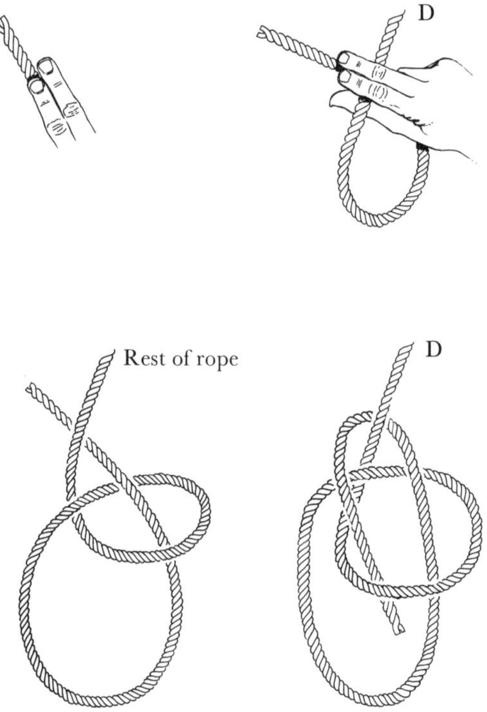

Fig. 27. The Bowline.

1. Lay two fingers of the right hand along the end of the rope with your thumb under the rope.

2. Lay the end on the main part of the rope, catching D with your thumb underneath.

3. Turn the right wrist *out* and form a loop with the end sticking through.

4. Pass the end round D and down through the hole again.

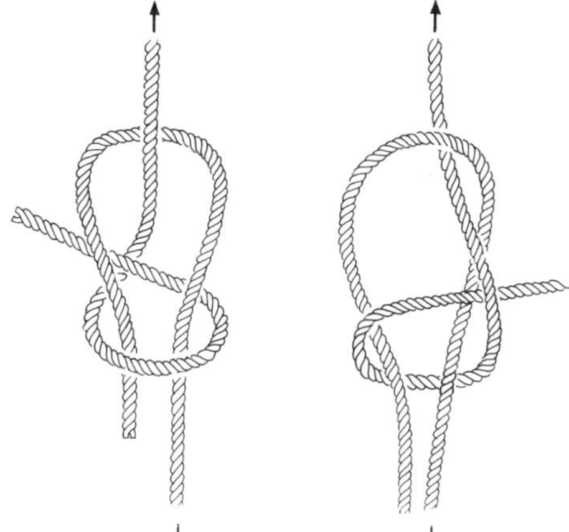

Fig. 28. An 'exploded' view of both sides of the sheet bend.

Figure 28 illustrates how to complete a **Sheet Bend**, which is for tying together two ropes of different diameters. It is tied in exactly the same way as a bowline.

The Figure of Eight Knot. This is for stopping a rope running through a block, and should be tied in the end of every sheet on board. It is so simple that I will leave you to work it out from Fig. 29. Start in the same way as for bowline and sheet bend (1), turn it round D and stuff it down the loop.

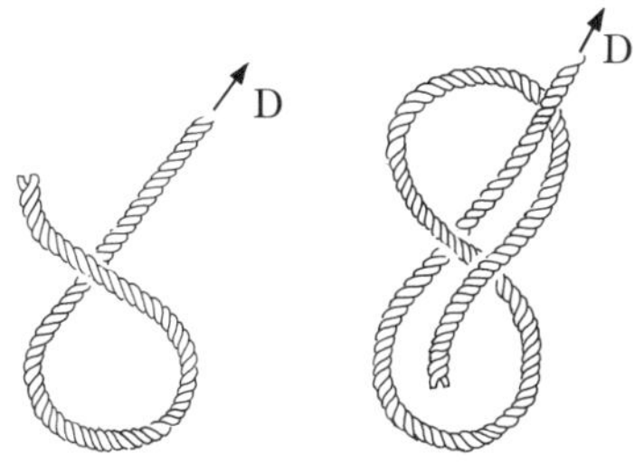

Fig. 29. Figure of Eight.

Make fast to what?

This section dealing with making fast would not be complete without reference to the objects to which you make fast. On the jetty you will find rings. You will also find bollards – and I have illustrated two kinds, single and double:

Fig. 30. Bollards.

There are also numerous 'cleats' to which you will be required to attach ropes, warps, sheets, etc. Note: *never finish sheets on to a cleat with a hitch like this:*

Fig. 31. Hitch on a cleat.

However, do use a hitch for other ropes.
Also much used is a 'fairlead', which is shaped like this:

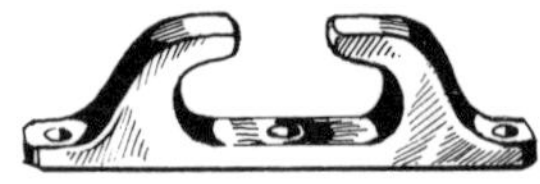

Fig. 32. Fairlead.

58   It stops any rope sliding about, or rubbing on your gunwales.

When attaching anything to anything else, sailors use a variety of shackles. The more usual one, illustrated in Fig. 33, has the bar capable of unscrewing and removal. There are also things called snap-shackles, which are of many different designs (Fig. 33B and C). Finally we have bottle screws (or rigging screws) which, when screwed up, shorten – and hence tighten – the rigging, or *vice versa* (Fig. 33D).

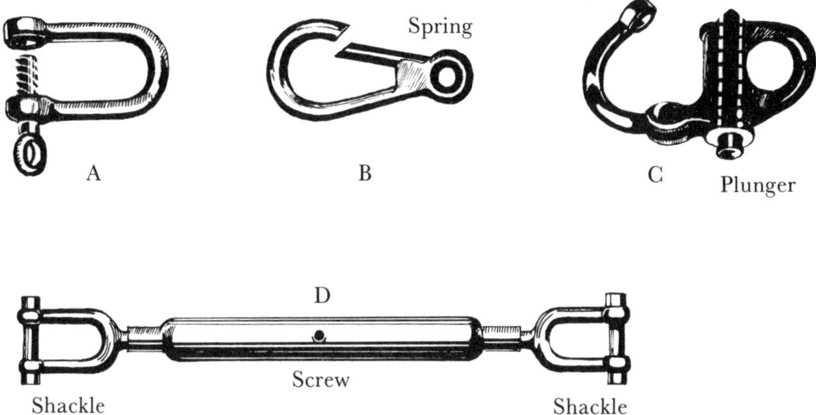

Fig. 33. Shackles (A, B, C) and a bottle screw (D).

4. Safety-wise

Where are the brakes?

Contrary to widespread belief there *are* brakes on a sailing boat. The basis of the braking system used is IF YOU DON'T USE YOUR FUEL, THEN YOU WILL STOP. There are two methods of stopping. Just as an aeroplane will stall if it tries to climb too steeply, if you try to sail too close into the direction of the wind, you will stop. So, if you *want* to stop, turn the boat up into the direction of the wind. Look up the mast at the flag. Once you are experienced you will not need to – and should not – look at the flag (properly called a burgee if it is triangular). But on this occasion you may. If its point is aimed directly over the middle of the back end of the boat, you are steering the boat directly into the wind. The sails will not fill with FUEL.

Alternatively you can do the job more quickly, by means of what I call PANIC STATIONS! You just let go of both the sheets and the tiller! The sails themselves will immediately turn their leading edge towards the wind, the boat will stop and the sails, being loose, and not restrained, will act just like the weathercock on an old church steeple. The boat will eventually turn up into the wind and there we all are, upright, with flapping sails, and plenty of time to sort ourselves out.

Motor-boats are much the same . . . only different!

If the FUEL runs out and the engine stops, drop anchor and the motor-boat will ride quietly to her anchor. In fact, boats at anchor will ride to whichever is stronger, the wind or the tide. The majority of boats on moorings will turn their bows to the tide. So, when you next see some moored yachts you should be able to tell whether the tide is coming in or going out.

Going backwards and making leeway

I have already emphasized the necessity of knowing whether the tide is ebbing or flowing, going out or coming in, going down or coming up (they are all the same). I would like to say something more on this subject, which I hope will help you to 'orientate' yourself. Tide speed plus your boat speed = jolly good speed, BUT, against the tidal stream, the sum is: your boat speed *less* the speed of the tidal stream. This could mean that you are sailing hard to stay in one spot or, worse still, going backwards. You will still *feel* that you are going forward unless you can relate the path of the boat to something static like a piece of land.

Making leeway is somewhat similar; the action of the centre-plate and hull, in providing resistance, has already been described, but no keel is absolutely efficient. Your boat will be pushed sideways by the wind and certainly by the current in a river, or the tidal streams of the sea. The whole thing is, again, a question of relativity.

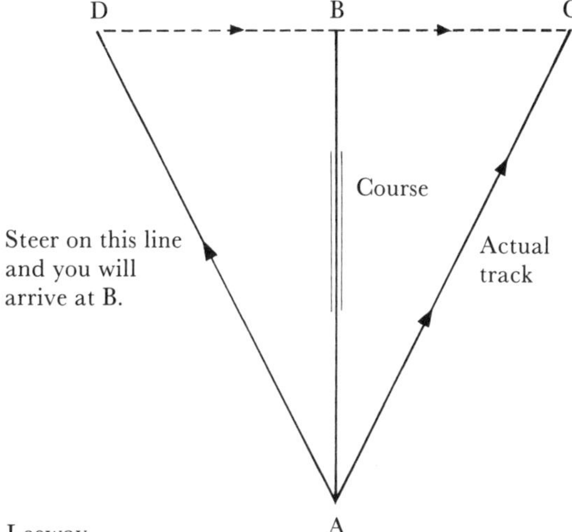

Fig. 34. Leeway.

You can be 'set down' by the tide (a sort of moving carpet effect) or you can make leeway. These are similar – but different. However, the simple diagram (Fig. 34) explains them both. Without any 'interference' your course would be from A to B, but with either 'set' or 'leeway' interfering, the actual track will be AC.

Clearly, therefore, to reach B you will have to compensate by steering along the line AD.

In a small boat, good judgement will be sufficient. In a larger craft this judgement turns into navigation, because of the larger distances involved and the fact that you are sometimes out of sight of land.

At this stage – and provided you don't capsize – you should, WITH PRACTICE, be able to get anywhere once you are launched and once you have used your senses to sort out what your FUEL is doing. Later in this book I will be describing the procedure for getting your boat off and on to the shore. It may seem illogical not to deal with these procedures first . . . but *before* leaving the shore it is vital to understand the basic points which I have so far described, otherwise even leaving the shore is a mad, disorganized scramble.

Talking of scramble, let's now upset ourselves and see how we can sort ourselves out when we do capsize – and we *will*, at some time! However, first some advice about lifejackets and buoyancy aids. You will need one or the other before you start capsizing.

Lifejackets or buoyancy aids

This is a lengthy subject, and for more detailed information there is an article on it, prepared for the *Royal Yachting Association Magazine* and available from the R Y A, called *When A Body Is Immersed*.

Briefly, there are lifejackets with some solid buoyancy, which can be further blown up to give 35 lb. buoyancy, sufficient for adults to float with head well clear of the water in a good position.

Plate 5. The Author and Commander Ian Sothcott discussing various kinds of personal buoyancy during the filming of the Thames Television programme

There are also jackets which are totally inflatable to the same limit but the first is better for children. Then there is a whole range of buoyancy aids which, in fact, *are* jackets with built-in buoyancy often on the back as well as the front. They are fine for use in sheltered waters.

A lifejacket, of course, looks like a horse's collar and is NOT a jacket! Most of the best ones are marked with the 'kite mark' of the British Standards Institution.

Good buoyancy aids look more like a waistcoat, laced or zipped up at the front. Many of these are approved by the Ship and Boat Builders' National Federation.

You can also buy harnesses with very long cords which can be shortened. They are rather a good idea for tethering the young and making sure that you don't have to fish 'junior' out of the water, and are essential equipment even for adults on board larger vessels on coastal or ocean passages.

Most of the qualified canoeists that I see around are also very conscious of safety gear and wear a very efficient buoyancy aid which does not get in the way of their arms when they are paddling. There are also one or two good makes of lifejacket which are recommended for canoeists. The British Canoe Union is one of the best organized bunch of 'boaters' that I know – so write to them for information on 'what to wear in the canoeing season'.

Capsizing in a canoe

Assuming that you have been idiotic enough to start off in a canoe without proper instruction, there are one or two interesting points worth mentioning. In the first place, if there are two of you in one canoe, don't try to change places except on land. Also, watch out for larger craft. You are very small to the observer from a few hundred yards away.

Suppose you do capsize, you will have to get out, and if you can't do the Eskimo roll, pull the 'panic strap' to lift the spray deck and forward-roll out.

An upside-down canoe will have an air pocket and very little water in it, so it will float, having buoyancy material in it anyway. If help is near, get help, but if it is not, don't try to climb on to the upturned canoe. The effect of this will be to spill the precious air out of its pocket and the canoe will become very heavy and full of water. Rest in your lifejacket or buoyancy aid and hold on to the canoe.

A

Plate 6. The self-help technique of
the Eskimo Roll

 B

C

If you are at sea – and there should be *at least* three canoes in company – it should be possible to right your canoe with the help of the others. The best rescue craft is another canoe, so I am told by a B C U coach. There is a special drill for righting a canoe which consists of getting under it (into the air pocket) and with a quick LIFT and THROW turning it upright without filling it with water. If you merely roll the canoe over, it will fill with water. This is surely another special technique which canoeists should learn.

The experts also indulge in a manoeuvre called the Eskimo rescue, or better still, the Eskimo roll (the 100 per cent self-rescue technique). The Eskimo rescue involves staying in your canoe when you go upside down and, because you can't right it, you signal by slapping loudly with your hands on the outside of the bottom of the canoe. If everybody is wide-awake, you will soon receive the bow of a canoe in one of your hands, which will provide you with a lever to right yourself. The great advantage of all this is that your canoe is immediately seaworthy since you have not undone your spray deck and let the water in.

The Eskimo roll is, in my opinion, a technique to be learned and then practised and practised and practised. Once capsized, the theory is that by pulling your paddle across the surface of the water 65 at a slight angle, and using your body and hips, you can 'flick' yourself upright. A combination of all three – paddle, body and the hip flick – will make the canoe rotate and you will come to the surface for a breath of fresh air.

Capsizing in a sailing dinghy

The National Sailing Coach, in his *Sailing Manual* for RYA instructors, presents the very best method of sorting yourself out in a small sailing boat which you have failed to keep upright. The tendency in nearly all today's designs of dayboat seems to be to carry as much sail as possible and 'right the boat' when it capsizes. In my view it is – for the 'cruising' man in any sort of sail boat – cleverer to reduce sail by 'reefing' or even put up smaller sails.

Reefing, incidentally, consists of pulling down the mainsail part of the way and rolling it or wrapping it on to the boom. In this way you present a smaller triangle to the wind.

In fact, in big sailing craft you can do both. A big sailing cruiser, if 'over canvassed' merely 'lies on her ear' and is *hopelessly* inefficient because so much of what is meant to be in the water is actually out of it. The boat is heeled over so far that she is using part of her deck as a hull. In that case, a reefed mainsail and smaller jib will allow her to stand more upright and, therefore, sail more efficiently.

I appreciate that in a small boat it is often difficult, if not impossible, to carry a number of sails – and difficult to reef the mainsail.

However, if you *have* capsized in a small boat, here is the drill for getting upright again, reprinted from *The Sailing Manual* by Bob Bond by kind permission of the author, the Royal Yachting Association and Messrs Pelham Books Ltd.

There are many factors which dictate what should be done in the event of a capsize. Whatever else happens, contact with the boat must be maintained, so that, should the need for eventual rescue arise, the crew will be with the most identifiable object, the hull of the upturned boat. For our purposes, we shall consider a capsize in moderate wind and wave conditions, such that a practical routine will result in a successful righting. The object of the righting sequence in a training programme is to ensure that beginners will accept a capsize as an integral part of dinghy sailing. It is as well to remember that boats were designed to be sailed, and a capsize is a potentially dangerous situation, especially so when the practice of sitting on the side of the boat, to keep dry, results in an inversion over the unfortunate crew.

This detailed sequence does away with the need for immediate lowering of sails and unnecessary positioning of the boat by swimming. In its entirety, it provides the novice with a logical progression of actions designed to get the boat upright and sailing in the shortest possible time. In a modified form it can be used by the racing helmsman to continue sailing within a minute of capsize.

In the sequence, the helmsman and crew have specific tasks. In the event of the crew being much heavier than the helmsman their roles should be reversed. We have assumed that the mainsail is transom-sheeted (i.e. the mainsheet is at the stern).

Stage 1: When the boat capsizes the helmsman and crew fall into the water on the same side as the sail. After checking that neither is caught in the rigging, both make their way to the stern retaining contact with the boat.

Stage 2: The helmsman checks that the rudder is secure, the crew *frees* the mainsheet.

Stage 3: The helmsman moves to the back edge of the centre-board, placing his arms over it to steady the boat (Fig. 35).

    Note 1   In rough weather the mainsheet is used as a safety line until the helmsman is secure at the centre-board.

        2   If the centre-board is not down, the crew will move into the boat and push it into the lowered position.

Stage 4: The crew finds the jibsheet and throws it over the side of the boat to the helmsman who acknowledges its receipt.

Stage 5: The crew lies in the boat facing downwards, his body supported by the water, knees on the inside of the gunwale (Fig. 36).

In boats which have large side tanks, the boat will float very high. It may be necessary to climb on to the side of the tank, clear of the water. This will help sink the boat and make Stage 7 easier for the helmsman. The crew may need to hold on to the toe-straps or centre-board casing.

Stage 6: The crew tells the helmsman everything is ready.

Stage 7: Using the jibsheet, the helmsman climbs on the centre-board as near the boat as possible in order not to snap the centre-board, which he would do if he stands on the end of it! Then he leans back pulling on the jibsheet. The boat will 'unstick' slowly. As it comes upright, the crew is scooped up (Fig. 37).

Stage 8: The boat is upright, the crew, having waited for the boom to swing over his head, scrambles to his feet.

Stage 9: (a) In boats with good freeboard, the crew rocks the boat towards the helmsman, grabs his hands and rocks back, hauling him aboard. (b) The helmsman may be able to climb aboard unaided as the boat comes upright. (c) In heavy boats, or boats with little freeboard, it may be necessary for the crew to bail the water before the helmsman comes aboard.

Stage 10: Helmsman and crew bail out the water and then sail away.

Note: CENTRE MAINSHEETS: Boats with centre mainsheets are seldom used for basic instruction or for practising righting techniques. We have tried various methods and recommend the following.

After Stage 1 all the crew's activities are carried out aft of the mainsheet. In Stage 5 the crew positions himself in such a way that he can grasp the centremain, or toe-straps, so that, as the boat comes upright, he is scooped up into the aft cockpit.

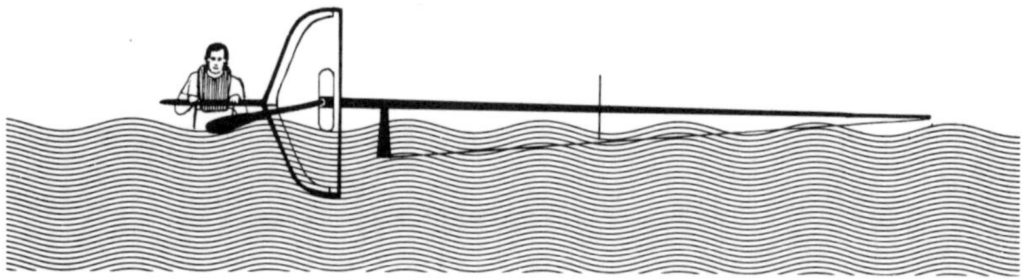

Fig. 35. Stage 3: helmsman puts arms over centre-plate to hold boat steady.

Fig. 36. Stage 5: the crew lies in the boat face downwards, waiting to be scooped up.

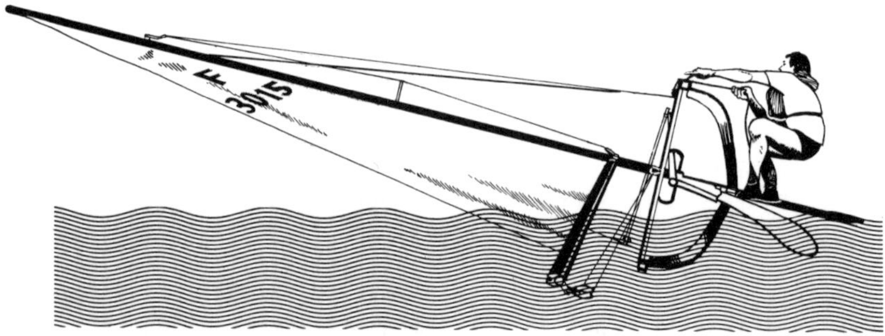

Fig. 37. Stage 7: having received the jib sheet from the crew, the helmsman puts his weight *close* to the boat and heaves on the jib sheet. This should unstick the boat and the crew is scooped up.

Man overboard (sail or power)

Let's talk now about the situation where somebody, somehow, has left the boat by accident. In larger boats, the lifebuoy, of which you should have at least one, goes over the side IMMEDIATELY. This is your first job, and should become instinctive.

There are many different ways of coping with 'man overboard' but, in a small boat without engine, probably with only *one* member of the crew left on board, it is safest to turn the boat on to a reach from *whatever* point of sailing you were on – e.g. if beating, ease sheets and the boat will soon be under control. Then go about through the wind (tack, in other words) and return on the line of your wake. It is unlikely that you will be sailing a small boat at night but count as you turn the boat on to a reach and, when you finally turn, count the same number back. By that method you should get into sight of that tiny head bobbing in the water.

I cannot see much wrong with this advice even for the lone wife whose husband has gone overboard from the larger family cruiser. However, so many people seem to think that you must *gybe* at once and follow the sequence in Fig. 38, that I begin to feel that one should not disagree. Either action will do but it has to be QUICK. Perhaps the best and quickest for the lone wife is to put on the engine!

What is certain is that you and your crew must learn how to cope with your boat so that any of you can bring it back to a definite point and stop it RIGHT THERE in an emergency. And be able to do this in a hurry without flapping. *This requires practice.*

Having got back to the man in the water, bring the boat into the wind, downwind of him. Judge carefully when to let the sails 'weathercock', or when to shut off the engines.

Picking up a 'man overboard'

If in a dinghy, drag him over the side of the boat – *not* the stern which is usually covered in sharp objects.

If on a cruiser or motor-boat there may be a good three feet of freeboard (distance between deck and water level) and the man to be rescued is most likely heavy with waterlogged clothing. The problem is how to get him on board?

In my view, *without a ladder*, the quickest and neatest method in a sailing boat is to lower a rope or sheet into the water in a loop, make fast (tie) the end to something (preferably a cleat) near the

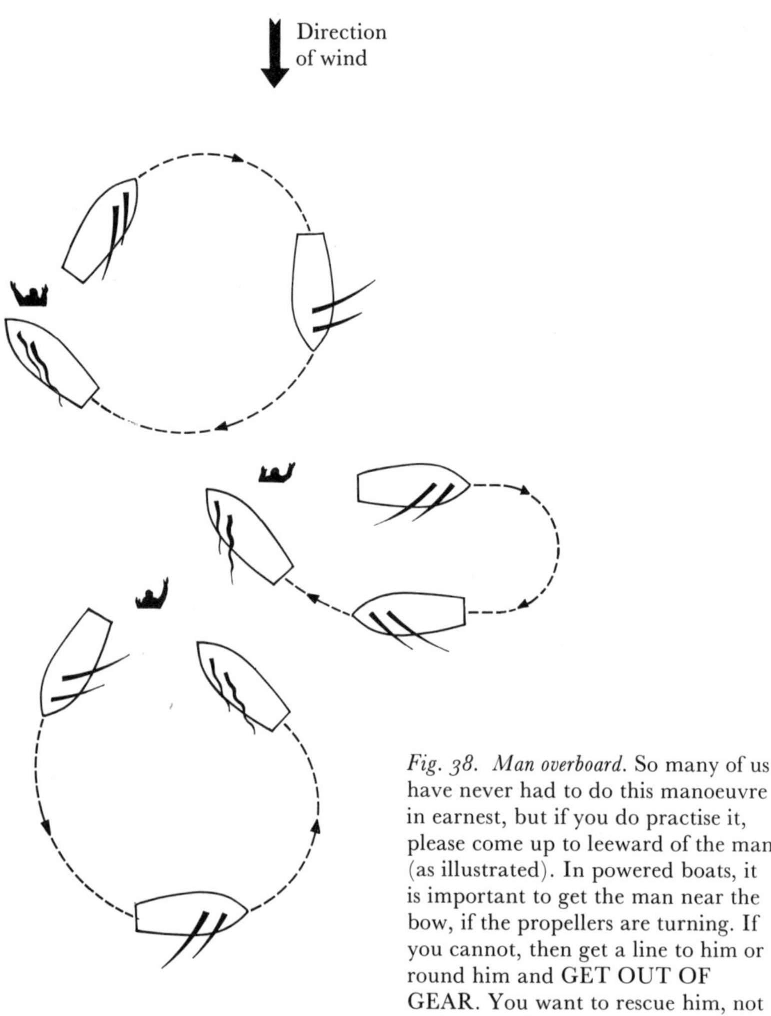

Fig. 38. Man overboard. So many of us have never had to do this manoeuvre in earnest, but if you do practise it, please come up to leeward of the man (as illustrated). In powered boats, it is important to get the man near the bow, if the propellers are turning. If you cannot, then get a line to him or round him and GET OUT OF GEAR. You want to rescue him, not cut him to ribbons.

stern of the boat and put the other end on a winch. The man in the water can then grab this loop and step into it, and you can winch him out if he is conscious. If he is not you will have to think of something else – AND FAST! Hopefully there are two of you left on board, so *your* crew, whilst you have been getting back to the man overboard, should have detached the jib halyard and bent on a loop of rope to the shackle. Slip this (easier said than done) over the unconscious man and winch him out of the water. If all this sounds difficult, be assured that it is! *Carry a rope step ladder and*

70

all becomes easier. The real trouble is that almost everybody thinks this emergency can never happen to them. The BEST way of dealing with a man overboard situation is to see that it never arises, by insisting on safety harness for *everybody* including the helmsman in anything like bad weather – AND AT NIGHT.

The most dangerous time is when the crew first come 'on watch'. Their eyes are unaccustomed to the dark, etc., so they should have a place to clip on their safety harness line even *before* they leave the shelter of the hatchway. The prudent skipper attaches 'dead-eyes' in strategic places and rigs a lifeline fore-and-aft, especially in smaller boats with guard rails and stanchions inconveniently situated to bend a chap's knees if he stumbles.

On any type of powered cruiser there is everything to be said for having a fixed ladder at the transom (stern) of the boat, so that anybody in the water can, provided the propellers are not turning, climb back on board.

Incidentally, I said earlier that a lifebuoy should be the first instinctive thing to go over the side. Do NOT throw it *at* the man in the water; throw it near him. It has always seemed to me that to suggest the lifebuoy should have a line on it is O K in everything except a sailing boat. In a powered craft, you will see him go overboard, *we hope*, and can stop immediately. In a sailing vessel under sail, you really cannot stop at once, so the advantage of having a line on the lifebuoy seems academic. You hardly want to throw a tethered lifebuoy only to tow it away from your long-suffering friend in the water! Talking of him and the lifebuoy which you have thrown to him, I hope you will have taught your crew the correct way of getting into a round lifebuoy. It is *not* duck-diving and trying to come up inside it.

Swim towards it and grab the nearest side. Bend your head down, and flick the lifebuoy over your head, so that the furthest side of it is then behind your back. Bobbing up and down, trying to swim into the thing is vastly amusing in a swimming pool and HOPELESS at sea.

MANOEUVRING UNDER POWER

Most sailing cruisers have a propeller installed on or near the centre line, just forward of the rudder, to give maximum slipstream to the rudder. A rudder won't work without forward motion of the boat (steerage way) or backward slipstream provided by the propeller.

A

Plate 7. The helmsman rights a capsized dinghy in the approved style (Chapter 4)

B

C

D

Power cruisers sometimes have 'outboard' propellers which turn in response to the wheel and they act as motive power as well as rudders.

Single screw craft

The upper blade of a propeller works in less dense water than the lower blade. Propellers can turn either way, dependent on whether there is reduction gear between engine and propeller. Assuming that your boat has a 'left-handed' propeller (looked at from behind the boat), it will be turning anti-clockwise. Its effect (transverse thrust) is known as 'paddle-wheel' effect and it will tend to swing the boat's bow to starboard even when the rudder is 'amidships'. If you reverse the engine, the tendency will be for the boat's bow to swing to port, and this will be pronounced. Also, for those who drive a car it will come as no surprise to learn that when reversing, if you turn the wheel to the left (port), the bow of the boat will go to starboard.

Twin screw craft

The *majority* of twin-engined recreational craft have *both* left-handed propellers.

Whatever you buy, you must immediately find out which way the propeller or propellers turn. It makes all the difference to the way in which your boat will handle. Having found out this important fact, you will then have to practise like crazy. Of course, in a twin-engined craft, if you put one engine in slow reverse, and have the other one running forward a little faster, you can turn on the spot in your own length without touching the rudder. Very useful.

It follows that if you come in diagonally towards a jetty against the tide with a twin-engined craft you can (coming alongside port-side to) shut off your port engine, reverse starboard, even leaving your rudder amidships or slightly to starboard, and you will drive the stern of the boat quietly in alongside (see Fig. 39). There is no rush and if you have to pull out and start again, do so.

At slow speed the rudder does not *do* very much and, therefore, in twin-engined craft you *can* steer the craft by judicious use of engines only. If you do use the rudder, use it to suit the engine which is going ahead.

The modern motor cruiser *is* designed for 'planing' and there-

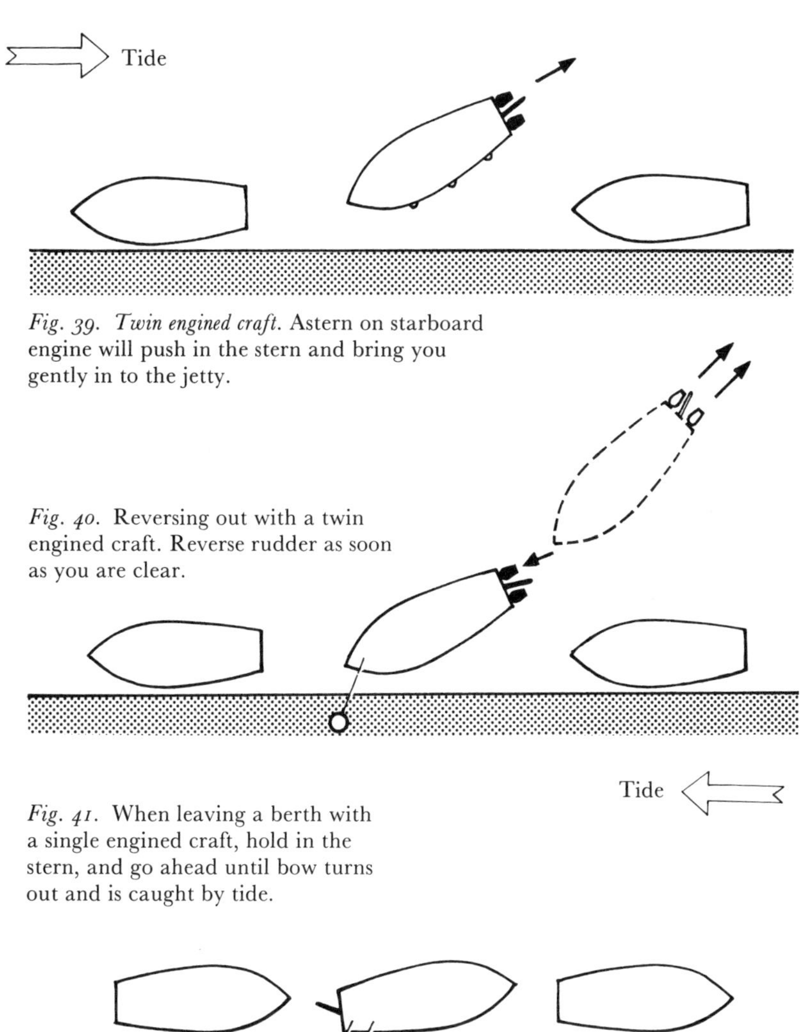

Fig. 39. Twin engined craft. Astern on starboard engine will push in the stern and bring you gently in to the jetty.

Fig. 40. Reversing out with a twin engined craft. Reverse rudder as soon as you are clear.

Fig. 41. When leaving a berth with a single engined craft, hold in the stern, and go ahead until bow turns out and is caught by tide.

fore is without much of a keel. It also often has quite high topsides upon which the wind blows, and it is this, as much as the tide, which may have the greatest affect on your decisions about manoeuvre. Almost invariably, with twin-engines, it is safer to leave by reversing out. There is such power that even a sluicing tide has little effect. In fact Fig. 40 probably explains it all, better than words. Protect your bow with a fender, leave the bow line on, go ahead on starboard, a touch on port in reverse, helm to port if anything, until you are 'tail out', then reverse the helm and set both engines running astern.

In single-engined craft you do *not* have the benefit of the 'skidding' ability. Coming into a jetty you must nudge in until the man in the bow can get ashore, turning your craft alongside and only reversing the engine to slow her up. You are relying on rudder and tide to turn her in sufficiently until the stern line man can get ashore as well.

When leaving a berth in a *yacht*, rather than a motor cruiser, you must use the tide to help you, because getting steerage way on to a yacht with a small propeller takes quite a long time. It may, in fact, be necessary to turn the craft round on the mooring before departing so that she will react as in Fig. 41. When leaving against the tide, hold your stern in, by a line ashore which you have brought back on board. Put the rudder hard over and when the tide (and stern line) have swung out your bow, let go, haul in and motor quietly away.

Tide-wise

In fact, the words HAVING APPROACHED AGAINST THE TIDE are probably the most important single lesson one can learn. The neatest way into a confined space is not necessarily a straight line! That is why you will see so many craft come in, apparently over-shoot the spare place and then 'round up' and come back, to go into the space you thought they had spurned. You *try* stopping a boat when the tide is hustling you along. Use the tide as a 'brake' by coming up into it, and giving a touch on the throttle as and when necessary.

What I have suggested about twin-engined craft going out astern can be varied to suit the occasion. There are many times when it will clearly be easier for you to hold in your stern, push her out, using the inside engine, and let the tide take the bow as in Fig. 41.

All this may sound incredibly complicated. The real answer is to think out your problems before you start, and tell everybody on board what you intend to do. *No shouting* when leaving or arriving. It is remarkable how quietly it can be done when everybody is 'clued up' as to the helmsman's intentions.

Coming alongside

You should decide which side the crew are to put out the fenders, and tell them to do it *long* before you actually come alongside. If you have a spare (and relatively inexperienced) person on board, give him a roving commission with a fender in his hand and tell him to hang it over whenever he thinks your boat is likely to bump into another. In most small craft it should be unnecessary to hurl coils of rope at the bystanders. A crew member at the bow should 'make fast' the end of a rope to a cleat on board and the stern line man does the same. Then they each pass their coil under the guard rails and through a fairlead (if there is one) and are ready to step ashore, with coil of rope in hand, as you nudge in the bow. The stern line man should pass his line under the guard rails where the line will eventually lead when you are docked. Then he should walk forward, passing the coil outside everything to about half-way up your boat. He is off the boat and on to the quay only split seconds after his 'mate' in the bows. You meanwhile are going barely at steerage way.

Before your men go ashore, you should tell them to leave the lines slack, unless you have too much speed on. They *can* do a quiet bit of holding back, if they see your bow going too near the boat in front. You will thank them for it later.

I have deliberately assumed that you are coming alongside another boat or a pontoon. What you will often find, in locks and harbours, is a jetty or quay at which the ground level is higher than the deck of your boat. Then your crew, in a temporary situation, has to slip a line through rings or ladders on the wall and bring the line back on board. They can then 'play' the line as necessary, 'paying out' as the water level rises in a lock or as you manoeuvre alongside the jetty.

Mooring up

Now to the question of how to tie your boat up for the greatest safety and convenience of all concerned including other boat owners. Basically Fig. 42 explains the method for all types of craft.

A and B hold your boat to the land or to piles (posts) in the middle of a river. C and D stop your boat from swinging away from the next-door boat, or the quay, and then BANGING back again. E and F stop the forward and backward sliding motion, which rolls your fenders constantly back and forth and probably catches your rigging in the chap's next door. Very expensive! Springs (E and F) should be lead in a straight line from the bow of one boat to the stern of the other (or the quay) and the second spring is, of course, t'other way about.

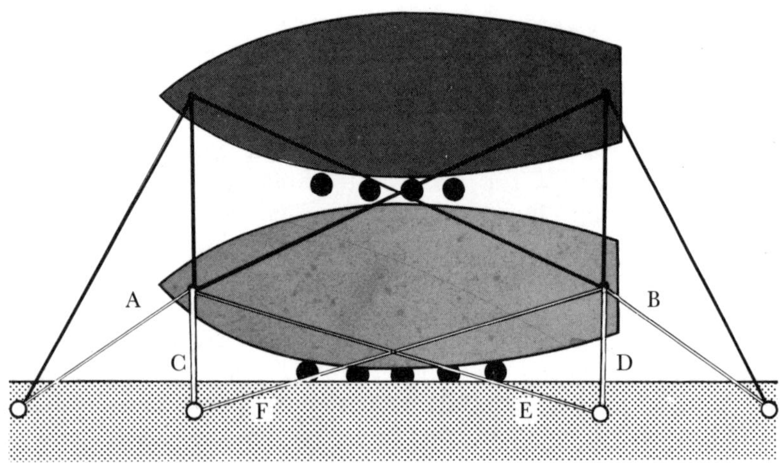

Fig. 42. Mooring lines. The lines A and B are bow and stern lines, C and D are 'breast ropes' and E and F are called 'springs'. The outside boat does N O T rely on *your* warps. He should put out his own to the shore. He will have to remove one or the other if you want to leave before him, B U T it is his duty not to rely on *your* mooring lines. The weight of his craft and yours may be too much for your warps only.

In a harbour where there is a big rise and fall of tide, your warps and springs must be lead as far forward and aft as you can possibly manage. When the tide rises and falls they will have quite a large 'radius'. The breast ropes are the nuisance. Clearly they must be left slack, off, or constantly attended – otherwise, when the tide falls, you will be using the sides of your yacht as the floor and the bunks; you will be on edge – and your mast will be forming a temporary barrier across part of the harbour!

The courtesy of the sea

Logically, I should now deal with anchoring, but I am going to assume that this is something more associated with deep water and deal with it later. Meanwhile you have arrived amongst other people. You have to be careful of your property and theirs. You have also to be careful not to offend, or inconvenience, your fellows. With that in mind, put out plenty of fenders and use them till you are clear away. On the sea, never leave them dangling over the side, because you will lose them. Get them inboard and stowed *as soon as you are clear of the mooring area.* They are so easy to forget.

On rivers and canals, they may need to be permanent fixtures because of the frequency of locks, etc.

Talking of safety, inconvenience, etc., there are one or two general points worth mentioning:

SAFETY FIRST

Gas cookers can blow your deck off, and others nearby! Always check the gas taps, as you do at home, and turn off the BOTTLE COCK when the cooker is not in use. Gas tends to sink, being heavier than air, so you could be standing on a bomb under your cabin sole.

Fuel is just as dangerous – and we need so many different kinds on board. All should be clearly marked, in suitable containers – and only a very few plastic containers ARE suitable. Diesel oil in the bilges is unpleasant and petrol is not to be lived with, nor put in the kettle by mistake!

If there was room I would go on repeating this next remark about fuel, wherever I mention engines in this book:

Everybody on board should know where to turn off the fuel supply to the engine. In case of trouble with engine control, it is the first thing to do.

Your children at sea are really vulnerable. They should not be allowed to sit on the bows, where you can't see them. One bounce on a wave, and over they go past the hull towards the propellers. Equally, they should not be allowed to play about on the stern, or indeed anywhere on deck. NOBODY should be on deck longer than it takes to do the necessary job and return to the cockpit. Above the roar of even a small engine, a child calling for help may not be heard. At sea, and even on river craft, children should be both HEARD and SEEN. Adults, if they have to go on deck in anything like nasty weather, should have one hand for themselves (hanging on wherever possible), and should also clip on those life-harness lines in really rough conditions.

Rubbish. This should not be thrown into the sea, or in inland waters. Polythene bags can be sucked into an inlet and stop an engine, and string or rope from a parcel can wrap round a propeller. Old bottles and cans can cut feet on the beach. Only food for the fishes should go over the side, and in inland waters not even that. If every boat threw away two pounds of rubbish into the sea on Saturday and Sunday in the Hamble River alone, that would amount to just over six tons of rubbish floating on the tide each week-end. So do take it ashore, and dump it in the bags or bins provided at most marinas – or even take it home and put it in your own dustbin!

Accidents and illness on board

The more people who know something about First Aid the better. However, even if you don't, you can take some sensible precautions if you are taking the family away in your newly bought family cruiser (power or sail).

Clearly, near water, *somebody* should know how to resuscitate the apparently drowned person. Immediate action saves lives and you can't wait for the doctor to arrive. Consult your local St John's Ambulance Unit, or the police. Even find out from the local school how to do the mouth-to-mouth method of resuscitation. It is important.

A major danger is seasickness. The will to 'carry on' is badly eroded by this malady. Then the rest of the crew get exhausted, because some are 'off watch', lying in their bunks. There are pills for seasickness, some of which make you sleepy, which is not good. Please experiment, until you find the one which suits you.

Burns, cuts, scalds and sunburn are the other usual problems. A First Aid box with burn dressings, antiseptics, ointments and plenty of bandages and elastic plasters suffices for everything except broken limbs. The briefest advice on these is to immobilize the patient and make for the land.

Remember also that food kept on board can do strange things. With no 'fridge', do see that you don't serve up meat and other perishables too long after they have been purchased. They seem to go bad quicker when kept in a locker on board.

It is rather dreary to keep hammering on about all the deadly things which can happen to you if you dare to take to the water. It is in fact not a dangerous sport IF YOU KNOW OF THE PROBLEMS – so here is one more for you:

Cold can kill

I have already referred to the necessity for taking warm and waterproof clothing to sea in small craft. The same applies in larger craft. There is a very good article by Surgeon Commander Walters of the Institute of Naval Medicine which was first published in the magazine of the Royal Yachting Association and is constantly reprinted. It is well worth obtaining a copy. Walters points out that the *core* of your body must be around 'normal' temperature for you to be comfortable. Your skin may, and will, vary in temperature, but the deep body temperature should not drop below 35 °C (95 °F) otherwise you are likely to feel the effects of *hypothermia*. Clothing keeps the wind out, and the hot air in, and that's why you should wear a windcheater (anorak or oilskin). The insulation value of clothing when wet is less than one-tenth as effective. Wet suits (skin-tight 'rubber' suits) help to maintain your own private 'climate' and any clothing helps. It is a great mistake to believe that if you swim about you will keep warm. It has been proved that it is much better, if heat conservation is the aim, not to replace your own private climate with cold water by swimming about madly.

If your crew start shivering in the boat they are on the way to hypothermia, so watch it. Progressively they will become listless, lose interest, fail to obey an order, etc. As they deteriorate they will see less well and become confused. Now, this is not a joke, it is a serious warning. It *happens* even *out* of the water so do watch it. If you tip your crew into water of around 5 °C (41 °F) the average chap will be helpless in less than half-an-hour. On board, sea-sickness adds to heat loss and should be avoided by doses of hyoscine. If you have been immersed for long periods check your crew and re-warm them as soon as you are ashore. Briefly, a hot bath is the best way of recovery. Better still, never let it happen.

5. Seamanship and Equipment

Your craft should be equipped according to the *International Regulations for Prevention of Collision at Sea*. The Regulations stipulate the navigation lights and sound signalling equipment that should be carried. Here is a check list of other equipment:

1. **Safety harnesses** for each man on a cruising yacht.

2. **Lifejackets** for everybody (a 'buoyancy aid', which is less buoyant than a lifejacket, will be adequate in sheltered waters).

3. **Lifebuoys**, if the craft is big enough. These, for obvious reasons, should be in easy reach of the helmsman.

4. **A small dinghy or rubber inflatable.** In larger craft the specially packed inflatable life-raft is also necessary. See that the oars and rowlocks for the small dinghy are handy.

5. **Anchors** (plural!), with rope- and chain- (well sufficient for the depth of water in which you are operating). Three times the depth of water is a rough guide to the minimum length of rope required, and the anchors should have eighteen feet of chain to help the anchor bite into the ground.

6. **Bilge pumps, buckets or bailers**, according to the type of craft. If you have bilge pumps check that they work. They can be jammed by a match – and often are!

7. **An efficient compass** (and a spare, probably hand-bearing, one, as well).

8. **Charts**, *at least* for the immediate area in which you are likely to operate.

9. **Distress flares.** MINIMUM two red flares, but it is better to have at least six, two of these being of the parachute type. (Please read the instructions on flares as soon as you buy them and see that the crew do so as well. It is a bright prospect if you let them off upside down!)

10. **Distress smoke signals**, for daytime use.

11. **Tow rope** (especially for motorized craft). This should be of adequate length and diameter to take the strain of your craft.

12. **First Aid box** (including anti-seasickness remedy).

13. **A transistor radio** (for listening to the weather forecasts).

Plate 8. A full equipped club rescue boat, illustrating what *should* be carried on board even a boat of this size

Plate 9. The modern yacht harbour provides many services but the yachtsman must still ensure that his vessel is equipped for less comfortable situations

14. **A water-resistant torch**. Even in daylight, the engine compartment is very dark.

15. **Spare ropes** to use as lifelines, or for other uses.

16. **Engine tool kit.** This really is vital. On land most of us don't carry a full set of tools in the car. At sea, where salt water 'eats' the engine, and there are no mechanics or AA men, *you* must have the proper tools.

17. **Spare sparking plugs.** A new sparking plug can work wonders on an otherwise silent engine.

18. **Spare shear pins or springs.** These are for outboard motors and really are vital. Read the manufacturer's instruction book, together with the section about engine maintenance in this book. Your goose is cooked without these tiny spares.

19. **Spare winch handles** (see Chapter 6).

20. **Radar reflector.** On craft which can carry them in the correct way these may save being 'run down' by a big chap. If the radar reflector is merely hung in the rigging it will be *some* good. Better still to hang it up correctly.

21. **Fog signals.** Even the smallest craft should be able to make its presence known in fog. The tiny aerosol fog horns have quite a good range. On larger vessels you can really go to town with a big 'grunter'.

22. **Oilskins and warm clothing, adequate food and drink** (especially water!).

Fire on board

I am not merely going to *list* fire extinguishers, because there is much to say on this very important subject. First, you are stupid if you don't carry them. Fires can be started by corroded electric cables, by fuel, either engine or cooking, and by many other causes.

The 'cleanest' extinguishing material is the inert gas BCF (bromo-chlorodifluuoro-methane) or BTM (bromo-trifluoro-methane). Keep out of the compartment into which you fire the extinguisher. The fumes could overcome you.

Foam and powder extinguishers are, in my view, second best because they make such a devil of a mess, but they are equally effective as extinguishers. The real fact is that you should have a number of extinguishers on board. Do not try to put out a fuel fire with water. Petrol and oil float on water and you will simply float the fire further round your craft.

84	In the case of fires feeding solely on wood, wool, sleeping bags, etc., water can be used but there is much to be said for the proverbial 'wet blanket'. It smothers the oxygen upon which fire flourishes.

Navigation lights

This is another item which deserves more than mere listing. Because it is last upon my list, do not think that it is unimportant. If you are out at night in your car, you carry lights. Why anybody should think that it is any less important to do so at sea, is quite beyond me. In a sailing craft, see that the battery is charged up properly. If it is not, then run the engine, to keep the lights up to the maker's specification. A 12-volt battery, which is sagging, may give less power, and by the time the electricity has travelled along all those wet and old cables to the bulbs at the 'far end' or up the mast, you will have lost even more power.

There is no excuse for any sort of powered craft to be badly lit because the generator is running all the time.

The Collision Regulations tell you where, and what, lights should be displayed but, to simplify it, a small sailing cruiser should carry lights which show in 'sectors' as in Fig. 43.

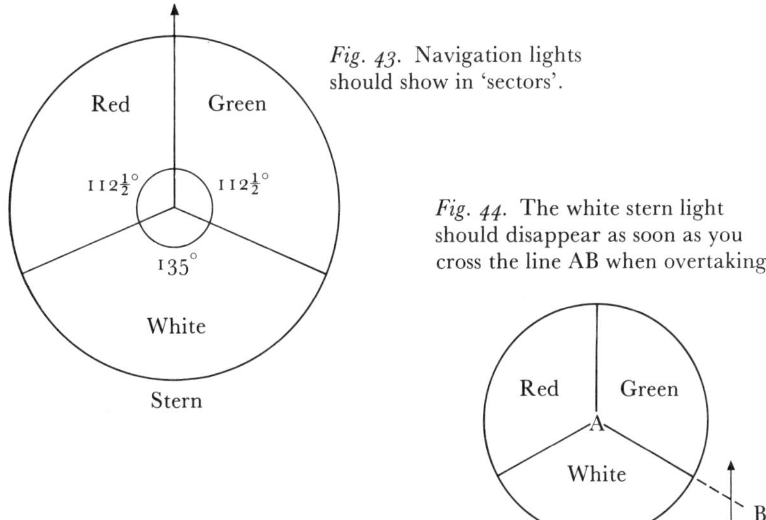

Fig. 43. Navigation lights should show in 'sectors'.

Fig. 44. The white stern light should disappear as soon as you cross the line AB when overtaking.

If you are under power you must show the same lights *plus* a 'steaming light' which shows through BOTH the red and green sectors. I do not like the yachtsman who pretends that his 'all round' white light at the masthead will work as a steaming light AND a stern light. If you are following a powered craft, or a sailing vessel, you will see one white light at the stern until you have nearly overtaken her. As you can see from Fig. 44, what SHOULD happen is that the white stern light 'disappears' as soon as you cross the line AB, and the green light will appear. There is an absolutely marvellous 'picture book' called the *Seaman's Guide to the Rule of the Road*. If it is unobtainable at your bookshop write to Teaching Programmes Ltd, Bristol Tutor Group, Mark Lane, Bristol 1. I have spent many happy winter evenings trying to answer the questions it poses without looking at the answers. I recommend you to do the same, rather than try to remember funny little rhymes for every eventuality.

Rules of the road

We are, at the time of going to press, using the 1960 Edition of the *International Regulations for Preventing Collision at Sea*. There will be a new edition in a few years time but meanwhile there are no changes to the rules as set down here. You should, however, be careful that you have got the most up-to-date edition because the 1960 Edition DID change the sailing rules a bit. The rules are designed for all types and sizes of craft. Both you and the super-tanker are subject to them. The steering and sailing rules are designed to give everybody strict rules to ensure that *when in danger of collision* there can be no doubt about where you steer. Because we do not all 'boat about' all the time we have to *think* and to help you to do so here is a little 'rule':

Left, **Port** and RED are short words and go together (and Port-wine is Red!).

Right, **Starboard** and GREEN are long words and they go together.

Here are two basic rules:

'When in doubt STOP', and 'KEEP TO THE RIGHT'. We drive on the roads on the left and we do <u>not</u> on the sea. The third basic 'rule' I personally would add is that: *all pleasure craft beware* of commercial shipping. This makes sense in view of the difference in size, especially in narrow channels.

86

Plate *10*.   Port and starboard – whose right of way? This pictures illustrates the absolute necessity of knowing the Rules of the Road

Plate *11*.   When two power-driven vessels are meeting end-on each shall alter her course to starboard so that each may pass on the port side of the other

Also, POWER gives way to SAIL.
These rules are for *close quarters situations* – so if you see another

powered craft two miles to starboard don't cross over just so that you can pass him on the 'correct' side!

However, WHEN TWO POWER-DRIVEN VESSELS are meeting end on, or nearly end on, *so as to involve risk of collision,* each shall alter her course to STARBOARD (right) so that each may pass on the port side of the other (Fig. 45).

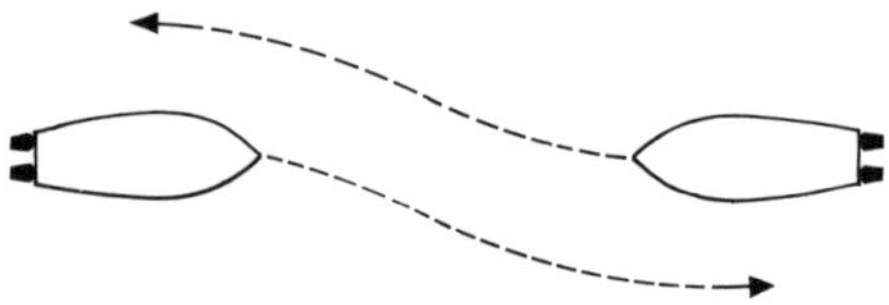

Fig. 45. Power meets power.

The next rule which is important is: when two power-driven vessels are crossing, *so as to involve risk of collision,* the vessel which has the other on her own starboard side shall keep out of the way of the other (Fig. 46).

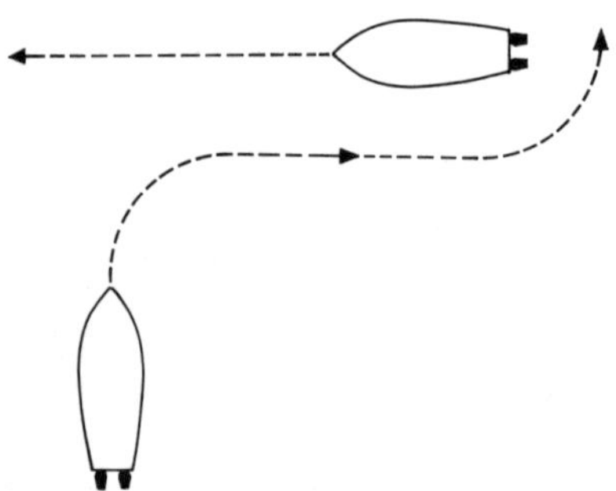

Fig. 46. Power vessels crossing. The craft with the other vessel on her starboard side shall keep out of the way, preferably passing astern.

Now let us examine the rule for sailing vessels meeting each other: sit in your boat and LOOK TOWARDS THE BOW. The right-hand side of the boat is the starboard side and the left is the port side (left and port are four-letter words!). If the wind is blowing on the starboard side of your boat, your boom will be over the port side – YOU are on starboard tack. You ask yourself, 'Which side is the boom?' and the answer is that you are on the 'opposite' tack.

1. Bear this well in mind. You meet a vessel which is on the opposite tack to you. If YOU are on STARBOARD TACK you have right of way and he must avoid you (Fig. 47). I quote: 'When each has the wind on a different side, the vessel which has the wind on the PORT side shall keep out of the way of the other.'

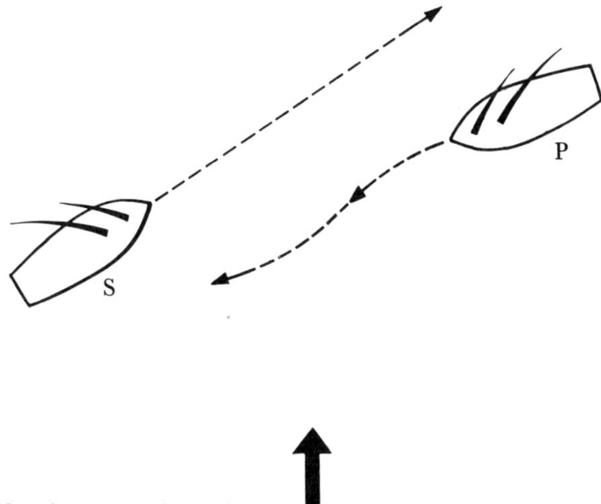

Fig. 47. Vessels on opposite tacks.

2. When both vessels have the boom on the SAME SIDE the vessel which is nearer the wind KEEPS OUT OF THE WAY (Fig. 48). I quote: 'When both have the wind on the same side, the vessel which is to WINDWARD shall keep OUT OF THE WAY of the vessel which is to leeward.'

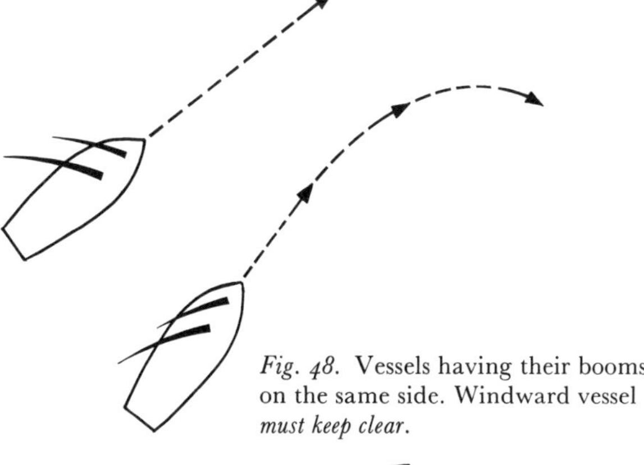

Fig. 48. Vessels having their booms on the same side. Windward vessel *must keep clear.*

3. Any vessel which is OVERTAKING another shall keep clear (Fig. 49). Actually the rule is a little more complicated but for all your purposes it is best to say 'he probably hasn't seen me so I won't, when overtaking, go too near him'.

Fig. 49. Overtaking vessel, *under power or sail*, keeps clear.

4. POWER gives way to SAIL (because he has more capability of manoeuvre). BUT this does not mean that you can expect a supertanker, which takes ten miles to slow down, to alter course for you. Since you are likely to meet these commercial vessels in narrow waters you are not only advised to get out of the way, there is a rule about *you* in the *Collision Regulations*. So keep out of the light of the big stuff; he might run aground avoiding you.

LAST BUT NOT LEAST, IF YOU ARE GOING TO CHANGE COURSE, DO IT FIRMLY, BOLDLY, AND IN AMPLE TIME SO THAT YOUR INTENTIONS ARE OBVIOUS.

Tidal consciousness

I spoke earlier of spring and neap tides. Now we must investigate, a little more closely, exactly what the effect upon your boat will

Plate 12. Keel boats racing in the Solent. Other pleasure craft should keep
clear out of courtesy

be, and the importance of the tides, whatever type of boat you
are using.

The table set out below shows, graphically, the various defini-
tions which will be helpful. Note particularly the difference
between 'range' and 'rise', and between 'springs' and 'neaps'.

In the first place, the tide does not rise and fall exactly the
same amount all the way round the British Isles – and in the
Mediterranean there's hardly any tide at all. Tide tables will
tell you what the tide is doing in your particular part of the world
on a certain day, and EVERY day is different. A tidal atlas will

Fig. 50. Range and rise

Mean High Water Springs (MHWS)

Mean High Water Neaps (MHWN)

Spring
Range

Mean tidal level. (The tide rises and
falls equally, above and below this line)

Spring
Rise

Neap
Range

Mean Low Water Neaps (MLWN)

Neap
Rise

Mean Low Water Springs (MLWS)

Chart Datum

tell you in what DIRECTION, and at what speed, the tidal currents, caused by those tides, will carry your boat so that you can adjust your course accordingly.

Range and rise

The rate of rise and fall of the tide is not constant. At high or low water, it is moderately slow, but at about half tide it is rising and falling rapidly. *Most* tides take approximately six hours between high and low water so you can roughly find the level at any given time by a simple rule of thumb:

Suppose the RANGE of a tide is 12 ft.

In the first   hour it will rise or fall 1 ft $= \frac{1}{12}$th of total
In the second hour it will rise or fall 2 ft $= \frac{2}{12}$ths of total
In the third   hour it will rise or fall 3 ft $= \frac{3}{12}$ths of total
In the fourth hour it will rise or fall 3 ft $= \frac{3}{12}$ths of total
In the fifth   hour it will rise or fall 2 ft $= \frac{2}{12}$ths of total
In the sixth   hour it will rise or fall 1 ft $= \frac{1}{12}$th of total

$$12 \text{ ft} = \tfrac{12}{12}\text{ths of total}$$

This is known as *The 'Twelfths' Rule*.

Remember it: 123 − 321.

Accordingly, if you beach your dinghy at the beginning of the second hour and return to it at the end of the third hour, you will find it further up the beach. How much further up the beach depends on the slope of the beach, but the tide will have gone down VERTICALLY 5 ft in that time! Equally, of course, if the tide had been *rising*, the chap who parked his 'Mini' on the sands and went off to the pub, might imagine it had been stolen. In a way he would be right . . . King Neptune at work!

Tidal streams

Whilst the tide has been going up and down, the tidal streams have been rushing back and forth. As you may, by now, have grasped, the tidal streams will be strongest around mid-tide.

A good lawyer is not the man who has all the information in

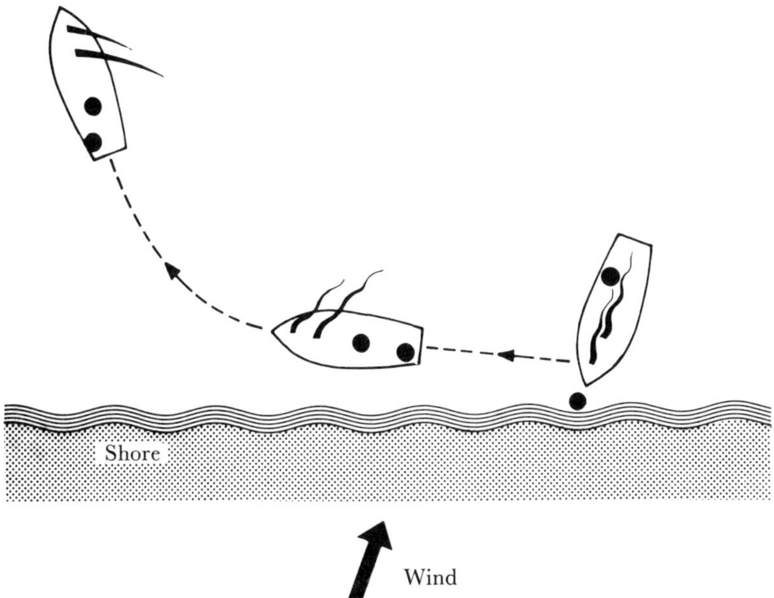

Fig. 51. Sailing off a weather shore (see Page 94).

his brain, but is the man who knows where to look for it! The seaman is the same. The signs are there for him to see. Buoys with the stream running on them will have a build-up of water on one side; craft at anchor will be facing the tide (more likely than not), etc., etc. If our boat is large enough, we will also have a carefully selected library on board. This will include *Reed's Almanac* (the yachtsman's bible), charts and tidal stream atlases even the *Admiralty Tide Tables*. These books will not last from year to year because the tides are never the same two years running, and charts need correcting.

Work your tides

With this amount of information available it is, I hope, clear that you have a lot to learn in order to use your cruising boat to the best advantage. If you are making a passage of eighteen hours' duration (say 120 miles), leave just as the tide is turning in your favour and you will have two favourable tides and one 'foul' tide. The difference in hours of travel is enormous if you plan it wrong and have two 'foul' tides and only one favourable one.

For your dinghy the 'speed' factor is just as true.

On the beach and off it

Talking of dinghies, we will now return, as promised earlier, to the subject of starting off from a beach and returning to it. This is not done by putting up the sails and simply floating off. We must think about where our FUEL, the wind, is coming from.

Wind from off the shore (a weather shore)

Put the boat in the water, hold the bows to the wind, and hoist the sails in peace and quiet. One person makes sure that the boat is head to wind and the sails will then not fill as you hoist them. When all is ready, the crew gets in and the helmsman turns the boat round, leaving all the sheets slack. Then, when he is in and all ready, you both sheet in a little and sail off downwind, with the centre-plate very nearly in the 'up' position (Fig. 51).

Sailing off a lee shore

There is, however, another – and very different sort of situation. Perhaps I should describe what a lee shore is, before I start telling you how to go about leaving it.

A LEE SHORE is one on to which the wind is blowing from seaward. If you are in a merchant ship, a large yacht or a motor cruiser and your motive power breaks down, see Fig. 52 for the likely consequences!

However, in a dinghy, you should have no cause for fear, especially since it will often be the case that you *must* launch from a lee shore. It isn't easy, but it is certainly not impossible. How do you go about it?

The crew holds the head of the boat into the wind – and this time he will be standing in deeper water. Get the sails up and fixed. Organize the boat with the centre-plate all ready to lower. The helmsman then holds the boat by the stern, still pointing it into the wind (he has to be strong). The crew gets in with all speed, the helmsman gives a mighty shove and 'throws' himself into the boat. Both of you sheet in and the crew (who has, of course, four pairs of hands!) lowers the centre-plate CAREFULLY so that it does not hit the ground and bring the whole operation to a grinding halt. The centre-plate is vital to give 'bite' and stop the boat just being blown back on to the shore again. Even the best crews sometimes make a hash of it. Fig. 53 shows what can

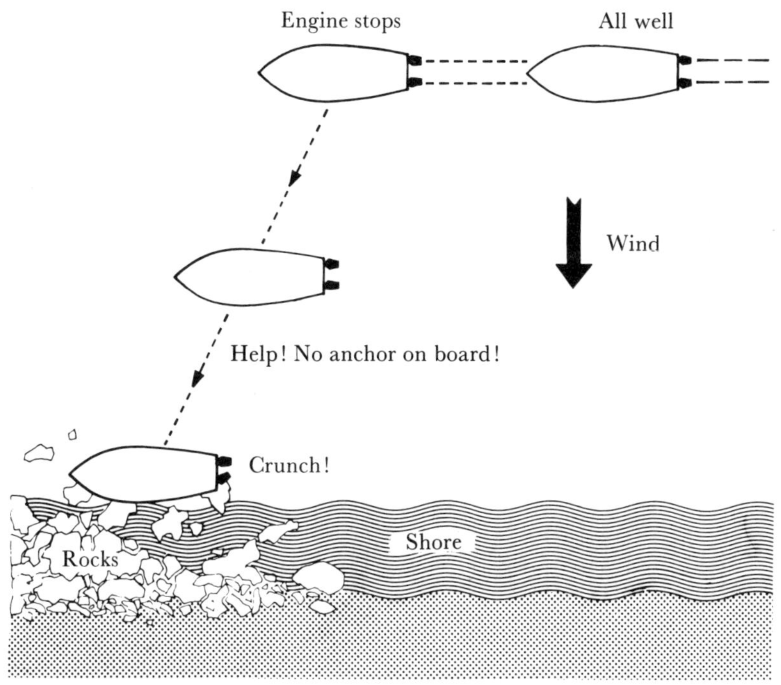

Fig. 52. Dangers of a lee shore.

Fig. 53. Sailing a dinghy off a lee shore.

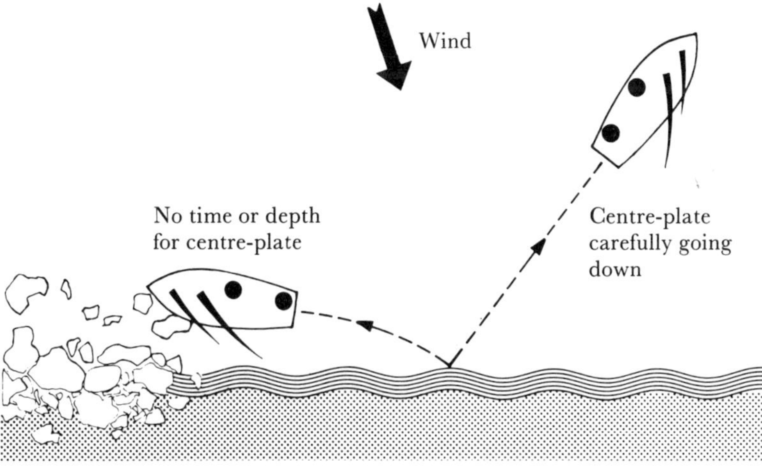

happen if you do not use your brains when choosing the tack on which to set off.

Coming home safely

Clearly if you come home to a lee shore under full sail when the wind is strong, you will arrive with a crunching rush. Under such circumstances, turn up into the wind well away from your beach, lower the mainsail, turn round again and sail sedately into the shore, letting the jib sheet go and perhaps even lowering it when you judge you are bound to reach the shore with no further motive power needed.

When arriving on a weather shore, you must organize your tacks so that you come in nicely under control, raising the centre-plate towards the last moments of your voyage and letting the sail 'weathercock' to take off your power.

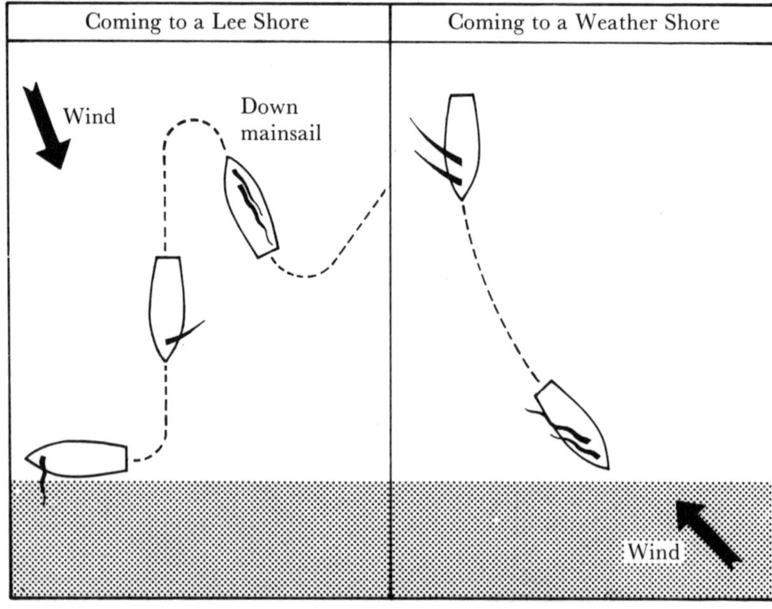

96   *Fig. 54.* Coming home safely.

Weather-wise

Reference to coming safely home to a weather shore prompts me to remind you again that the sea is quite oblivious to you! It does what it has been doing since the world began and it is like a spoilt child. It is unpredictable, unless you listen to the experts. One of the great troubles in using a small boat, is that a very slight change in the weather affects you enormously. So, find out the local weather conditions by any means in your power (see Chapter 2, perhaps even re-read it).

Use your eyes

I am sure that there are thousands of week-end sailors who are blissfully unaware that the 'black cones' displayed on the land denote that a gale is imminent – and that the way they are hung indicates its direction – though this is of little consequence to the small boat owner. A gale, of any kind, means that you should not go out.

Reed's Almanac gives many addresses from which you can obtain information but, frankly, you will soon learn a great deal from experience of watching the sky and then seeing what happens in the next few hours. On land you will note when it rains, etc., but on land you can also start learning to note what the *wind* does when the clouds and sky are overcast, or there are 'mares' tails' high up. Even the clearest of days can indicate what the wind will be doing. Every day at breakfast time, look at the weather and stop thinking whether you ought to take a macintosh to the office. Start thinking like a seaman. In a dinghy or open boat you are at great risk and really should not have ventured out. It is *your* fault if the helicopter has to come over to pick you up, and you are bringing the days of 'prohibition' nearer by your casual attitude and the underlying feeling that 'somebody will always turn up'.

You will say that I have painted a black picture and that I must be fussing. I am not! What I, and so many others, know is that you will frighten yourself many times during a life at sea. Sooner or later, preferably sooner, you will gain a healthy respect, but also a love for THE SEA.

Engines and their care

I shall be discussing in Chapter 6 *details* of engines but here I should like to say something about the largest single item in the coastguards' reports of rescue incidents. In only two months of one year there were over 250 calls on the rescue services – involving R N L I, coastguard and helicopters – to retrieve power craft and the people on board. If your lawn mower breaks down, it is inconvenient. If your boat engine breaks down, it is downright dangerous. Do take some simple precautions before untying the boat and setting off seaward, particularly if you are borrowing or hiring a powered vessel.

Inboard engines

1. As soon as you go on board a boat with an inboard engine, check the bilges (the hull space below engine and cabin floor). If there is a lot of water you can be almost certain that the 'seal' round the propeller shaft (where it passes through the hull) is weak. This means that you will be quietly filling with water all the time you are out at sea. Do NOT sail until it is mended (if it is really bad the boat may have to be taken out of the water). Most boats have a sort of remote-controlled grease gun which feeds this 'stern gland', as it is called, with grease. Give the poor thing its grease and you may cure the trouble, for the time being.

2. After the bilges have been checked, check the fuel and the sump oil. Remember the oil on your garage floor? There is equally no reason to suppose that a salt-eaten engine will always be full up with oil. Checking fuel also includes checking that vital reserve can. Somebody may have 'borrowed' it, since it should be clearly marked *Petrol* or *Diesel*.

3. Start the engine and check that the cooling water is circulating in, and splashing merrily out. Quite a number of polythene bags are found in engine cooling water inlets – and that could mean the end of the main bearings of the engine.

4. Check the throttle linkage REGULARLY. I know one owner who knew that his throttle spring was badly corroded, did nothing about it and, by a series of totally unrelated events, the net result was a bill for a new engine, repairs to the boat and payment to others.

5. If there is any way of checking that the petrol is not full of bits, or the carburettor has no sludge in it, please do that also.

6. Make sure that your gears work. The linkage is usually rather complicated and does need maintenance.

7. Check dynamo charge and belt drive for tension. Somehow on yachts, it always seems to be the belt that is slipping and the result is a flat battery. Ideal for starting the engine and for the navigation lights, don't you think?

Outboard engines

1. Check fuel and spare fuel can or tank – and remember that coming home against the strong ebb tide will be like climbing

a hill in low gear, with fuel being used up in double quick time.

2. Check all connections, linkages and cables.

3. See that you have spare plugs on board.

4. Check that you have spare shear pins or springs (according to the type of engine) on board. These shear pins or springs are situated behind the propeller and are *designed to shear* if the prop. is obstructed. Whilst it is difficult to replace one in a bobbing boat it is not impossible but it *is* if you haven't one with you!

5. In the case of a small boat which is 'rowable' in the event of trouble, check oars and rowlocks.

6. Check that you have your anchor on board (for when the engine does stop). The day before I wrote this I heard of a club *rescue* boat which drifted for miles after its engine stopped and the anchor was missing. It happens to the best prepared people. Somebody had 'borrowed' the anchor!

What to do in the winter

If the boat is to be left in the water all winter, you will have problems next spring unless you take some simple precautions. Preferably leave the engine in running trim and turn it over at least once a fortnight. If possible, actually run it for half-an-hour or so. This will mean that ideally you should remove the battery, take it home, and put it on a trickle charger. The next best thing is cranking the engine on the handle. If the boat is stored on land this is all you *can* do.

In any case, at the end of the season you should wash down the engine with fresh water to get the salt off, and pump out the engine bilge. The water cooling system is usually by 'heat exchanger' and most engines have fresh water in the actual engine jacket which is cooled by circulating salt water in the outer jacket of the heat exchanger. Some engines are directly sea-water cooled. If you can evolve a method of 'flushing out', all the better.

Then grease all linkages and lightly oil everything else. The petrol lines should be disconnected and 'blown through' because petrol lying in them tends to get 'tacky' and will not exactly allow 'free flow' next year. If you decide to empty the tank by siphoning, remember that petrol vapour is highly explosive. Allow the tank to 'air' before finally putting back the cap and going home.

   If you take the sparking plugs out of a petrol engine and put upper cylinder lubricant on the pistons, it will help to retard corrosion, or any likelihood of the engine rusting up solid.

Whilst there are many other things you can do, you should certainly read and follow the engine manufacturer's instruction book.

Outboard engines in the winter

Much of what has been said in the previous section also applies to outboards. Even if a tedious unbolting operation is involved it is not a bad idea to take your outboard home and service it.

RESCUE SERVICES

Assuming that you have taken all the precautions I have advised, do you then set off to sea without telling anybody where you are going? Does that really make sense? You may want to 'get away from it all' – but are you being responsible? What can a relative do if something happens that needs your attention urgently on shore? Many yachtsmen in larger craft can make contact via the radio which they carry, either Medium Frequency wavebands or the Very High Frequency (VHF) sets. Others – the majority because of expense – carry at the best an ordinary transistor radio.

You can also fill up the new coastguard CG 66 forms. One form is to give details of your craft so that the local Coastguard will get to know your boat. The second form is for longer voyages and sets out where you are going, and your track (or intended track). It gives a space for details of the crew and the equipment you have on board. In some cases this coverage from coastguard station to station will extend to some foreign rescue authorities. Each station will 'report' you as you go by. This is a good idea until you foul it up by changing your mind and darting into some obscure little anchorage. Then the whole service starts looking for you, especially if the weather is bad. If you make use of this service, remember, before you dip your nose into the next pint on some unscheduled stop, to ring the nearest coastguard, tell them and carry out the instructions on the forms.

If some anxious person reports you overdue, or if the services are looking for another yacht reported to be in trouble, it is also an excellent idea to make it easy for the helicopter to see who you are. If you can't stand the idea of painting your yacht's name large on the side of your hull, at least put up canvas screens to shield the cockpit from the worst of the weather (these are called 'dodgers', and very appropriately named) and then PAINT the name of your vessel LARGE and clear on the outside. Imagine a helicopter, propellers whirling (causing a downdraught), sneaking along up your stern trying to read the tiny name there. Another good idea is to give somebody on shore an EXACT description of your vessel – size, colour, rig, name, colour of sails, or type of power-boat engine, etc. We often hear that the coast-guard are having trouble because the only description of the wanted vessel they can get is: 'He bought it at XYZ three years ago. I think the hull is white, and there is a sail with some funny dead seagull symbol and a number on it!'

Towing or rescue by helicopter

If you are going to be towed home make sure that your craft will stand the minimum steerage speed of the towing vessel. If it won't, you would be better advised to abandon the yacht and accept a lift. This is tough advice, but a large vessel must maintain steerage way and this may be greater than your 'wee' vessel can stand without breaking up. If you do accept a tow, weight the tow-line. There are many ways of doing this but I think the best method is to make fast your strongest line to the shank of the anchor, pass the line to the other vessel and then feed out anchor and chain. Then make fast the anchor chain and spread the load to other strong points, besides the anchor winch – back to the sheet winches, on to the foot of the mast, even to the foot of the shrouds. The idea of the anchor hanging halfway along the tow is to absorb that awful snatching feeling (called snubbing) as the tow-line slacks and tightens.

Small boat towing

If you ever have to be towed in your dinghy or, for that matter, have to tow a sailing dinghy behind your power-boat, make sure that 'he who is being towed' brings the line through the 'stem' fairlead if there is one, or at least makes sure that the line, what-ever it is, comes over the bow of his boat. You should both be able to cast off quickly if anything goes wrong. In a dinghy, sit near the stern and steer the boat so that she does not sheer about and cause difficulty to the steersman of the towing boat. If a group of becalmed dinghies needs towing, it is best for one line to be streamed by the towing craft and for the dinghies to make fast by their painters on that line at regular intervals. There is nothing difficult about this sort of activity. It is much more difficult, as I have explained, to accept a tow in a larger pleasure vessel whilst at sea. Anyway, let's hope it never happens to you but if it does, you should think about possible salvage claims, which can be fantastic for very little.

Salvage

There are four cardinal rules:

1. Don't accept or ask for outside assistance unless it is essential. Whilst the RNLI and helicopters don't charge salvage there are others with an 'eye to the main chance' looking for suckers like you.
2. If you do, agree a definite fixed sum before accepting any help.
3. Don't allow anybody to come aboard to help you, and use your *own* line as a towing line.
4. The basis of any agreement should be 'no cure, no pay'.

You may think this is all rubbish, but I promise it is not. You should know the law of the sea, and salvage is a part of it. The Royal Yachting Association puts the law very neatly in one of their many booklets. Read it – and more. Even more important: make sure that you do not get into trouble.

Plate 14.   Even the most expert sometime need the help of the RNLI, the
         Coastguard or a helicopter

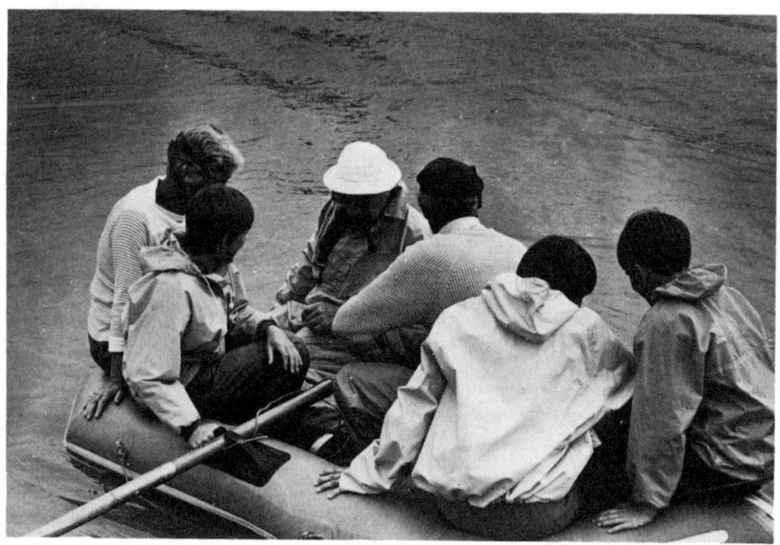

Plate 15. Several lives at risk in an overcrowded yacht tender

Actual rescue

What about rescue from a cruising craft? The R N L I Inshore Life Boat (I L B) is usually a rubber inflatable craft, with a rigid hull, and will arrive for small boat rescue at high speed. If you are further out, it is probable that the conventional lifeboat will arrive, or – quickest of all – the helicopter may come 'chopping' overhead. He will be looking down from a great height, so first of all indicate that it is Y O U who have somehow raised the cry for rescue. Fire off a rocket or flare, use a dyemarker, flash a light at him, lower the sails and wave the ensign about.

Your mast may be in the way of a helicopter rescue so it may be necessary for all of you to get into the dinghy, on a long line and drift away from the boat to give the winchman a chance to get at you. Anyway, for all ordinary purposes, let's suppose that the winchman indicates that he is coming aboard you. Clear as large an area as possible, push the boom over to the shrouds and lash it there. Above all, remember that the 'choppers' cause a terrific downdraught, and put on your safety harnesses, so that the winchman can grab you by something secure.

Distress signals

 Assuming that you cannot make the appropriate noises on the

radio, because you have not got one on board, there are any number of signals you can make to indicate that you are in trouble and need assistance.

1. You can fire a gun, if you have one, at intervals of about a minute.

2. You can sound your fog signalling equipment until you, or it, are exhausted.

3. You can fire off your red flares or parachute flares, making sure not to use them all up in the first minutes of panic.

4. You can morse S O S (dot, dot, dot, dash, dash, dash, dot, dot, dot) by light, or even by mirror if you are cute, and the sun is shining.

5. You can hoist the two International flags N C.

6. You can hoist, and this is the most possible, a square flag with a ball or anything resembling a ball, above or below it. Or the ensign upside down in the wrong place!

7. You can burn anything on board (not setting fire to your boat in the process!).

8. You can set off your orange smoke signal.

9. If you are very close to other vessels you can stand in a conspicuous place and slowly and repeatedly raise and lower your outstretched arms. If must be made clear that you don't just need the exercise and that you are not simply indulging in Physical Education. Who would be so mad?

Flags and signals

Having just mentioned the two flags NC, it is worthwhile to know that there are flags for each letter of the alphabet. You quite often see racing yachts with a single International Code flag used to denote which class they are racing in. The use of such flags otherwise *means* something. The latest 'code' was devised in 1969. For example, Flag F (white with a red diamond) means 'I am disabled, communicate with me'; Flag Q (plain yellow) means 'my vessel is healthy and I request free pratique'. Flag Q is therefore the flag with which you invite Customs aboard when you arrive in port from a foreign country.

It would take a whole book to explain all the meanings of even the single-letter signals. As soon as you proceed to the meanings of two-letter signals, I must refer you to specific books on the subject. Another opportunity for constructive reading in the winter evenings!

6. . . . *To be Forewarned and Waterwise*

I found a quotation the other day, which I now propose hopelessly to misquote, for it is the essence of this chapter. 'To know
what before us lies, is to be forewarned and Water Wise.'

Let's now assume that you are going to take the very great
step of acquiring a small cruising vessel, either sail or power, or
a bit of both. You are, I hope, going to look for a vessel approximately £300 less than you are prepared to spend. It will cost you
that and more, to equip her to the standard of safety which you
and your family deserve. It is not just a question of stepping into
a boat, all ready equipped, though some manufacturers are
getting to the point where they have, being seamen with a healthy
respect for the sea, provided a good inventory of essential equipment. If there is any justice in the world, they should sell more
than their competitors!

What, then, are you looking for when you go down to the
shipyard or perhaps walk round the Boat Show to see what is
there with an eye to purchasing something?

Is the boat suitable for your use and up to standard?

This chapter then is about using your boat and the way in
which she should be built, and equipped.

Anchors

You will perhaps have seen one or two small anchors, but what
is the 'best buy' for your 'pocket cruiser'? Not a fisherman's
anchor, nor the stockless anchor used on big ships, which tucks
away neatly into the hawse pipe. You buy either of the two sorts
of anchor illustrated in Fig. 55. Either are quite easy to stow on
the bows of a pleasure craft (power or sail). Personally, I find the
ploughshare shape (otherwise called the CQR) easier to handle
in a yacht. As it hits the seabed, it falls on its side and, as the pull
comes on the chain, it starts to come upright and buries itself
into anything but rocks. The CQR is nearly foolproof, but the

 Danforth also has many advantages. The stock prevents it landing

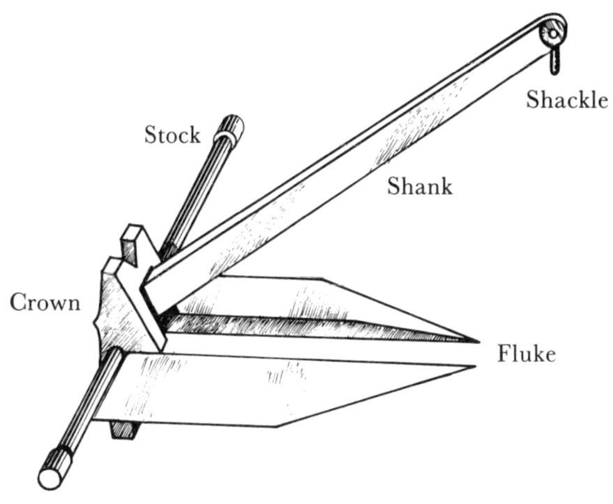

Fig. 55. Anchors. Above: Danforth;
below: C.Q.R. or ploughshare.

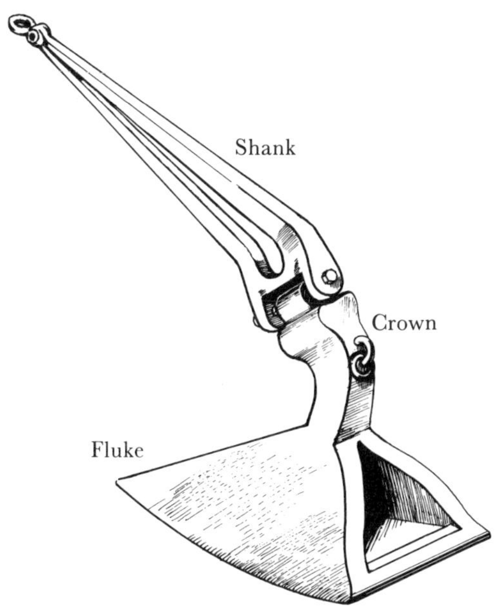

on its side and sliding along without digging into the bottom.

If you must settle for a rope, rather than full chain for your anchor, make sure it is nylon or terylene. Nylon has a nice 'spring' in it, and should leave you lying happily. However, all rope chafes at fairleads, etc., and chain is better. What you must do, is to have *some* chain at the anchor because it adds tremendously to the holding power. I said earlier that three times the depth of water in which you intend to operate was about right. I reckon that 180 ft of rope/chain (30 fathoms) is the absolute minimum. If it is chain, it will be led through a navel pipe on the deck, and down into the chain locker. The capping for the hole is VERY important. More water than you can ever imagine can get into your craft through there. Some caps have a slit in them, to accommodate one link. On others you have to unshackle the chain from the anchor and hang it on a hook on the underside of the cap. Anyway, make sure that there is a proper waterproof fitting. An old lump of rag won't do.

Dropping the anchor

Since your anchor, sooner or later, will foul an obstruction on the seabed, it is good practice to attach a 'tripping line' to the crown of the anchor. This is a length of strong line with a small buoy on it, which you chuck over, THROUGH THE SAME PLACE (over the stem of the boat) as the anchor will go. Your boat, whatever tide and wind are doing, should just be starting to drop back, as your crew lets go the anchor. Work it out to your best advantage. WHEN WIND AND TIDE ARE TOGETHER, you can round up into the wind. WHEN THEY ARE OPPOSED, you drop all sail and the tide will start to carry you backwards. That is the moment to raise a hand in a chopping motion for which your crew (wife?) is waiting. No shouting – because above the noise of sails, the anchor man may hesitate, wondering what you said. If your boat is *static*, all the chain will fall on the anchor, and *no* anchor will bite with a lot of chain on top of it. Be sure to let out an adequate amount of chain, ensure that the anchor has held in the seabed and, once all is settled, insert the pin across the stem head fitting through which the chain passes. This pin will stop the chain 'jumping' out and causing damage. Ideally, the stem head fitting should have a greased roller for the chain to run over.

You must also ensure that when you are in a crowded anchorage you lay your boat so that she will not be within swinging distance of the next boat. Boats lying at single anchor do not necessarily swing in the same direction as each other, because of back eddies or currents. The same is true of boats lying at swinging moorings, so you have to leave plenty of room.

If you have a really long 'tripping line', with enough slack to bring it back on board, then *bring* it back on board. You can hang the buoy up in the forward rigging to serve as the 'anchored' signal which you should show when you are at anchor. If you are going to anchor near a fairway in the dark, you should carry on board some white light to put in the forepart of your 'ship' to act as an anchor light at night. For the average week-end yachtsman, the 'all round' masthead light will do, provided that the battery will indeed last all night. Those who do navigate regularly at night may find it easiest to carry the ordinary old hurricane lamp. It is easy to hang, and, as its name implies, is made to stay alight in a hurricane, during which I pity you if you anchor. More about how to cope in heavy weather in Chapter 7.

Since I am a great believer in 'never do anything in a hurry' and 'belt-and-braces' I have often been ribbed for standing apparently contemplating the scenery, when I have anchored. In fact, scenery is the last thing that is passing through my mind, especially in a crowded anchorage. There are more important points to watch. Is the anchor dragging? Is it worth reducing the risk of incommoding or damaging somebody else? Is it worth putting out a second anchor in a crowded anchorage? Answer, usually, 'Yes'.

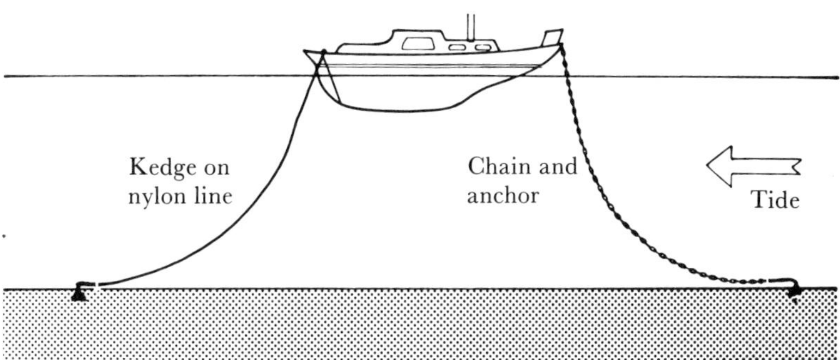

Fig. 56. Safely moored using two anchors.

There are many 'expert' ways of doing it. Perhaps the easiest, without leaving your boat, is to slack off the anchor chain and let the boat drop back *too* far, then put your second anchor over the stern, see that it is biting and take up slack on the forward chain again. Result, safely *moored* rather than anchored. This is a short-term idea, because when the tide changes you will find it uncomfortable to be stern to tide (see Fig. 56).

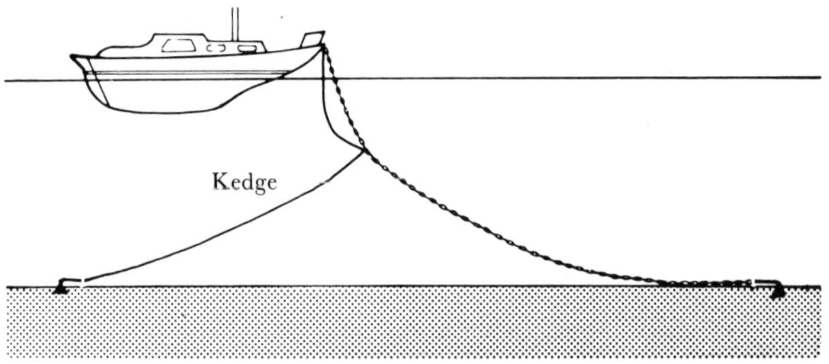

Fig. 57. 'Moored' to restrict your swinging circle.

I have supposed that you have *got* a second anchor. You certainly ought to have, at least, a light anchor (known as a kedge) on a long strong line. It is convenient to have this rope reeled on a drum. Amongst other uses you *can* sometimes pull yourself off when you go aground (which you will) by setting out the anchor as I shall now describe.

If you wish to 'moor' your boat, or 'kedge off' when aground, hang the anchor over the stern of the dinghy, flake all the rope into the bottom of the dinghy, or put your drum of rope in, tie the end firmly to your craft and row away, letting out rope as you go. Having set out the kedge, you should, when 'mooring', lead it from the bow, of course. It is sometimes advisable to go to even further trouble – raise the main anchor chain by a couple of fathoms or so, secure the kedge line to it with a rolling hitch and lower away again bringing the kedge line on board to make it fast. The net result of this wet and messy operation is that your craft is 'moored' by two anchors, on a shortened scope and she will have a very reduced swinging circle (see Fig. 57). I am told

 that you can get into a tangle doing this, though I never have.

The tangle is that, on the turn of the tide, the rope can get fouled up and you have to motor round your 'mooring' in order to unravel it!

Incidentally, if you *are* to be on your anchor through the turn of the tide (i.e. more than, say, five hours) it is good practice to lash your tiller (or wheel) over to one side or the other, so that the boat will turn round her anchor chain and not drag the chain across the anchor, with the possible risk of dragging it clear. As a matter of fact I was taught to give the boat a bit of a 'sheer' anyway. You only learn by experience but, before you settle down to that well-earned gin, watch everything closely to see that she isn't dragging her anchor. Your relative position to the shore-line and to other craft becomes rapidly apparent if you do a bit of scenery gazing. Perhaps the most important member of a big ship crew at anchor is the 'anchor watch'.

A 'fouled' anchor

That tripping line, about which I was talking (see Fig. 58), is attached to your anchor so that, if the anchor does 'foul' anything on the bottom (an old chain or, heaven forbid, a cable of some

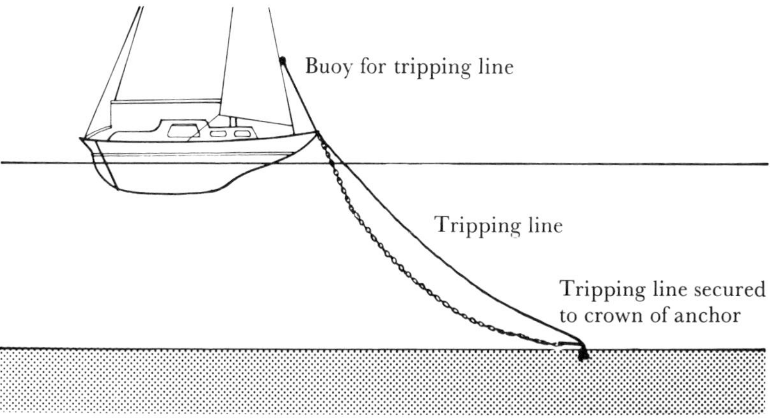

Fig. 58. A tripping line can be used to free a 'fouled' anchor.

kind), you can heave on the tripping line which, being attached to the crown, should draw your anchor fluke out from underneath the obstruction. If your tripping line fails you and you still can't shift the anchor, try to bring it *and* the obstruction to the surface, by winching and plenty of muscle power. It is hard work. If you manage, it is fairly easy to unravel and throw off the obstruction, ship your anchor and beat it for nicer places. If you fail, contrive a heavy ring of *something*, attach it to a rope and try sliding it down the fouled anchor chain. If it goes deep enough, you can row away with your rope and pull the anchor out forward. This 'heavy ring' can be merely a line, tied from crown to shackle of that second anchor which you are, of course, carrying.

As you will by now have realized, the best chance you have of not having to saw through the chain and leave your anchor for ever is to have that tripping line rigged.

Weighing anchor

The drill for weighing anchor is roughly the reverse of dropping it. If you move the head of the vessel forward, and shorten the chain, the ultimate result is that you will 'sail' the anchor out of the ground. Don't rush at it, merely move your craft forward as the anchor man lifts. If he has a hand free he can 'wave' as soon as the anchor feels free. Just hold the craft head to wind or tack a sailing yacht from tack to tack, whilst he raises the anchor well clear of the bottom until he can see it just below the surface. If it is covered in clinging filth go ahead, slowly, so that the movement can clean the anchor. Then give him time to bring the anchor right up. It is fairly critical to see that he has a fair chance not to bash a hole in your topsides as he brings it aboard.

Permanent moorings

Because we are all used to using pontoons, marinas or what you will, we tend to forget that there are many occasions when we will have to pick up a mooring. I must assume that the craft has an engine and yet, with a craft equipped with sails, the drill is hardly different. I have already said that to anchor, if wind and tide are together, you round up into the wind. Work it out for yourself, and practise bringing your craft to a standstill at a given point. Remember the number of frantic crew one sees trying to 'grab' a mooring with a boathook as the 'driver' approaches too fast.

It is tricky, though, because if you do it *too* slowly, just as the chap in the bow is within boat hook reach, the bow is 'blown off' by the wind, the vessel having lost steerage way. You need to practise it.

When wind and tide are opposed, you must lower the mainsail in a sailing vessel and work on the jib, dropping it at the correct moment to arrive 'delicately'. If the wind is blowing up your stern, under sail or power, you will have problems, especially with a mainsail hard up against the shrouds. Try it once!

Leaving the mooring

Check wind and tide. Look at the boat. Which way is its bow pointing? Under power, get your engines working, check everything TWICE, let her drop off the mooring, sheer away and put on enough power to clear yourself. In a sailing vessel, *if wind and tide are together*, hoist everything, 'back' the jib (hold it the 'wrong' side) and your bow will sheer away so that you can sail away on a close hauled tack. *If the wind is coming up your stern*, hoist only the jib, the tide will set you back as you let the mooring go, and you can chunter away under jib until you have space to turn the vessel up into the wind and hoist the mainsail. This fairly lengthy operation should be left until you are well clear of narrow channels. Most seamen will be *expecting* you to turn suddenly, but there are many on the water who do not understand sailing vessels. You can give a chap a nasty fright if you suddenly 'turn sharp right'.

The topping lift

In larger sailing vessels, other than small dayboats, the boom is so heavy that it must, when the mainsail is down, be supported by a line which runs from the foot of the mast, up the mast and down to the stern end of the boom. This is known as the 'topping lift'. Clearly when the mainsail is up, the topping lift should be slack to allow the sail to set properly. Before lowering the mainsail, see to it that the topping lift is taut and secured to its cleat on the mast, otherwise the boom will fall on to the helmsman's head, with unpleasant results for all.

Winches

In 'days of yore' and even now on sail training ships, there were no winches and the sails were sheeted on tackles, purchases and   113 with otherwise unassisted physical strength. For the small boat owner and his family, winches are essential. But what sort and size? Starting from the bow of the boat, I would suggest that, in anything but the smallest craft, an anchor winch, with dogs to accept the links of the anchor chain, is a good idea. Many a good back has been strained by too much anchor heaving. Equally the housekeeping becomes difficult if Mum slips a disc.

Then there must be winches for the sheets. For the small cruiser, I favour a top action winch (where you fit a cranked handle into the centre of the top of the winch). Once a 'week-end crew' get winding they can manage these very well. Of course, they will, from time to time, drop a handle overboard, or leave it in the winch until it *falls* overboard, so spare ones should always be in the Bosun's Locker (the odd 'bits and pieces' place).

It is a good idea to see that the winches are insulated from possibly reactive materials.

I have so often sailed in craft where the winches are too small (and you seem to wind for ever) that I *must* make the point that winches must fit the size of boat. It is a temptation (since they are expensive) to fit too small ones. In most cases you can only pray that the designer's specification is correct, and that the manufacturer wishes to sell articles fit for the purpose.

You must also see that the winches (port and starboard) *rotate the same way*. They should really be arranged to rotate clockwise because, apart from anything else, your crew will get 'muddled' at a critical moment if they do not. Winch mountings must also be strong. It is quite impossible to lay down the law, but see that they look workmanlike and are not 'perched' on a nasty bit of bent metal at the wrong angle for easy winding.

Use of winches

The actual use of winches is a matter of common sense. As the yacht goes about, somebody should be ready to flick off the jib sheet which will no longer be used. As the jib clew passes the mast, the sheet about to be used should be turned on to the winch with two turns and hauled in by hand as fast as possible. A good crew will need only a little assistance with the winch handle just to get the last of the sheet 'in'. If the crew is unfit one member can keep the tension on the 'tail' of the sheet whilst the other winds the winch. If the sheet starts slipping on the barrel of the winch, put on a third turn under tension (difficult over the top of the winch handle). The rope will then 'bite', and another little half-turn on the winch should finish the job. The sheet, still under tension, should then be 'made up' on to the adjacent cleat.

You will, when inexperienced, get many a 'riding turn' on your sheet winches. This is when one turn of the sheet 'jumps' over another on the winch forming a most efficient locking knot (since the sail is exerting such pressure on the sheet). This effectively stops all proceedings until it is cleared. It is worth learning the 'rolling hitch' or 'stopper' knot *just* for this eventuality. Make fast one end of a thinnish line to a convenient place, tie a stopper knot on the sheet, forward of the winch, slip off the riding turn and rewind the sheet properly on to the winch (Fig. 59). If the strain is parallel to the line of the sheet, the knot will tighten and

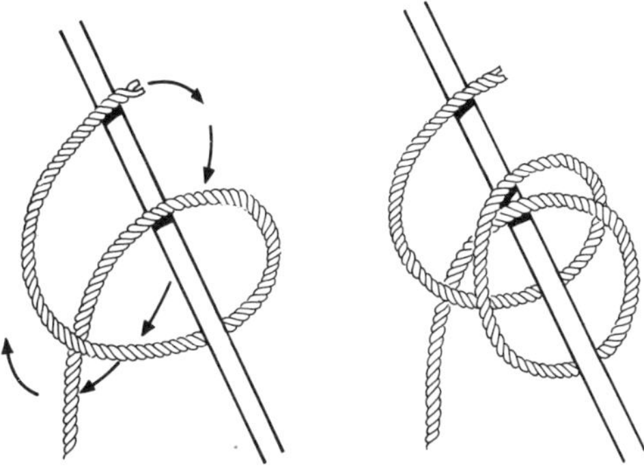

Fig. 59. The rolling hitch or 'stopper' knot.

hold for as long as you need. Of course, it may be that you won't need to go to all this trouble. You can, if cruising, go about, thereby freeing the sheet from its work and clearing the mess up as you go about.

SAILS

For the chap who is buying a boat which is primarily a sailing boat, the sails are important. You will certainly be sold sails made of synthetic fibres (generally called terylene). The days of cotton sails are just about over. Terylene sails do not mildew or smell, though it is certainly bad practice to leave them wrapped up or bagged in a very wet condition. You will often see a sail hoisted upside down – in harbour of course. This is an idea for drying them off, although I much prefer to see them 'weathercocking' the right way up. What you should always avoid is to allow a sail to slat about loose and uncontrolled for any length of time. It does it no good. The stiching and the shape can be damaged. If you must leave sails 'slatting about' take out the battens which can also cause damage.

Roller reefing

Because it is so much easier to reef a sail with the aid of roller reefing, the more expensive yachts will be equipped with this amenity. Don't imagine that it will *never* fail. Let me describe what I mean, *and* describe what reefing is all about.

Reefing the sails

The modern small cruiser is usually equipped so that, with yet *another* handle (apart from the winch handles), you can roll, from the mast end, the boom round and round. If the mainsail is progressively lowered as you do this, the sail will wrap round the boom, effectively reducing the sail area for bad weather sailing. As I have said before, a yacht with too much canvas will lie 'on her ear' and sail along with deck awash.

As you wind the boom round, also pull the sail towards the rear of the boom. This means a neat and effective roll, and will not pull the sail too badly out of shape. This is quite easy to do in harbour BUT suppose you get caught out at sea and the wind 'pipes up'. You set about roller reefing, and the gear jams or breaks. You can't then do anything except drop the sail and your position is extremely dangerous.

Here comes old man 'belt and braces' again. It is simple to have a row of reefing points sewn on to the sail and a couple of cringles (holes reinforced with brass) let into the luff and leech of the sail. Then, if the roller reefing does fail, you can simply tighten up the topping lift to hold the boom up, slack off the mainsail halyard, pass a stout line through the two cringles, drag the sail down and reef it in a 'slab' (or roll) with your thin reefing points. Fig. 60 shows roughly how it should look. It must not be tied round the boom unless it is essential because of design.

    Two vital facts about reefing. You *must* have more than one

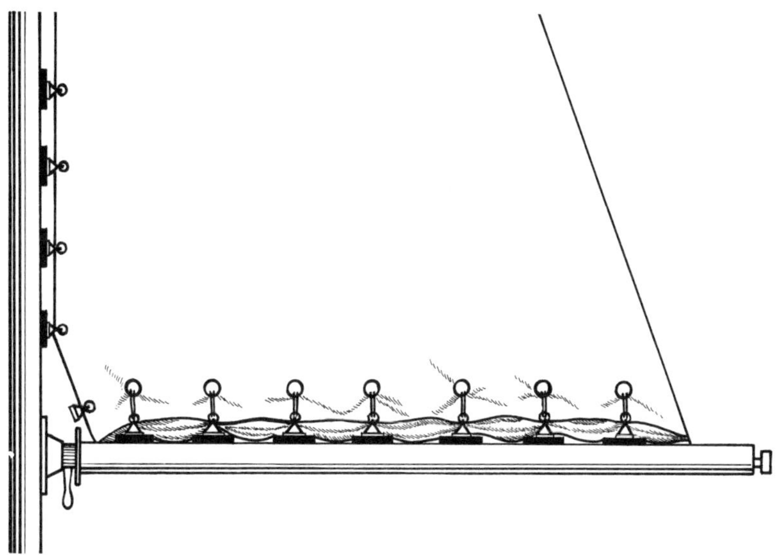

Fig. 60. An 'artist's impression' of a reefed mainsail.

foresail. A fair weather one (usually called a genoa) and a foul weather one (usually called a working jib). To reef the foresail, you change the size. Of course, you may have a roller reefing foresail. These are becoming more popular because it is probable that the cost of having a rolling jib-stay is cheaper than having (as many, many of the bigger yachts do) three or four foresails.

The *most* vital fact is that the prudent sailor 'reefs' according to weather predictions before he leaves harbour. So if you are warned of strong winds, reef the mainsail down before leaving. It is so very much easier to 'shake out' a reef than put one in at sea. And, of course, choose a small headsail if the forecast is bad.

The mast and standing rigging

Let us now look at the mast and how it is attached to the boat. In the first place, it is probable that you will be offered a metal mast made of alloy. These are less expensive to maintain than wooden ones but add to the initial cost. A wooden mast always needs a coat or two of varnish each year to protect it from the weather. I would always go for a metal mast stepped right into the bottom of the hull, unless I was going to use my boat where there are a lot of bridges. It often happens that owners want to use their engine up the canals and rivers of France, for example – 117 or even in Great Britain. If you are intending to do only estuarial sailing and a fair amount of inland water work, it is certainly better to have the mast 'stepped' in a tabernacle on deck. A tabernacle is a strong fitting to accept the foot of the mast with what amounts to a through bolt to keep the mast locked into this 'strong box'. It is then very easy for the mast to be lowered to go under bridges.

Whatever sort of mast you have, it has to be securely erected with the aid of forestay, backstay and 'shrouds'. These all should lead to good strong points, especially the shrouds which should run to a bottle screw (see 'making fast' in Chapter 2). The bottle screw should then be attached securely to 'chain plates' which in turn bear the full weight of mast and filled sails, so must be securely fastened into the hull. This has been an often repeated complaint in time past. The chain plates on some boats have not been strongly enough anchored to the hull. Galvanized wire and fittings are cheapest and are probably as trouble free as anything.

Stainless steel rigging must be accompanied by stainless steel fittings and this adds considerably to the cost. Rod rigging is a comparatively new but excellent innovation. I would only say that it is a little difficult to replace in an emergency, whereas wire is perhaps easier. It is also unnecessary for a small cruising boat to be so expensively equipped. Better to spend the extra money on safety gear or navigational aids.

Halyards

Except in the very smallest of boats, the halyards are made of wire and have a 'tail' of rope for you to handle and put round winches. You should check that when both halyards (jib and mainsail) are pulled really taut there is no rope on the winches. The wire should just be long enough so that, when the sail is FULLY hoisted up, there is enough for three turns round the winches, and a tiny bit over. The *rope* is then turned up on the cleat. To turn up wire on a cleat is bad practice, and bad for the wire which will kink and wear. Incidentally, always regularly check the splice where rope meets wire. The wire will also wear where it gets most strain, that is to say at the masthead block when the sails are fully hauled up.

Much of what has been said also applies to smaller cruising vessels, which may have rope halyards.

When you have hauled up the sails you will find that a vessel without halyard winches (i.e. the smaller ones) will still have some slack in the halyard and there is nothing worse than a jib with a sagging luff. If you tension the halyard under the cleat as in Fig. 61, you can 'take up' another good bit by 'swigging' the rope, three or four times. When you have all the spare rope in your hand, after hauling up the sails, coil it *from the cleat end*, pass your hand through the coil and grab the rope coming from the cleat, twist it through the coil and hang the whole lot back on the cleat by the twisted loop in your hand. Some people say 'fold the rope up and stuff it behind the halyard which will hold it in place'. Well, you can do that, but just see to it that, when you want to lower a halyard in a hurry, the spare is not all ravelled up and costs you

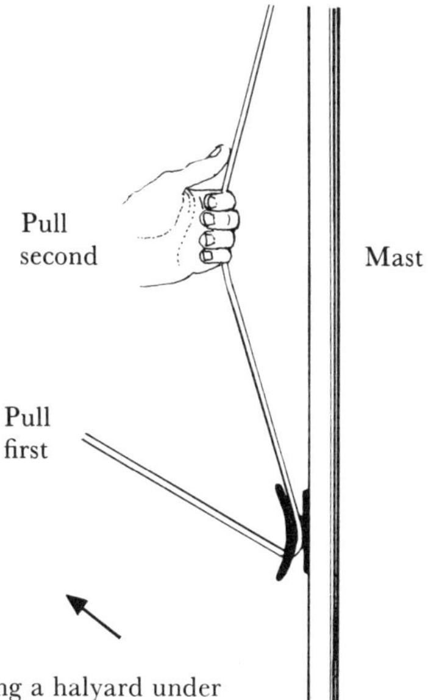

Fig. 61. Tensioning a halyard under a cleat.

time and trouble. What *is* most important is to ensure that whatever you do, there are no awful lengths of loose line kicking about on the foredeck to roll under the pressure of a sailing shoe or to trip up the unsuspecting crew moving, NOT running, round the foredeck doing their job.

FOR POWER AND SAIL

Because sail is a little more complicated than power only, I have spent some time discussing what to look for in a sailing 119 vessel. Now we come to what I hope will be useful hints and tips for owners of both types of boat.

Electrolysis

Various metals in sea-water atmosphere set up a vivid reaction against each other. The worst combination of 'reactive' metals is copper or brass, against aluminium alloy or galvanized material. They would be reasonably stable by themselves, though sea-water seems to 'eat' everything pretty fast.

Leaking electrical gear, like a cable which has lost its insulation, can cause a fitting to become negatively charged and it will eat away anything around it. Equally a metal fastening which passes through wood should be of all one material. Put a copper fastening through a galvanized fitting and you have trouble. On a steel-hulled craft, there are usually plates of special metal called 'sacrifice plates'. These are replaceable, after they, rather than your hull, have been 'eaten away'. They are indeed sacrificed. Since I was once scraping off the anti-fouling of a steel-hulled boat and the scraper went right through the 'steel plating' I can tell you that electrolysis means trouble. The best advice I can give is to get an expert to advise you and 'vet' the boat which you are buying.

Stowing the dinghy

When buying a boat I would hardly expect to buy one big enough to hoist a rigid dinghy in davits like a lifeboat on a liner! It is sometimes possible for a power-boat owner to do so, over the stern. For the majority of us, we have a problem, even with the rubber inflatable. Apart from the fact that you should really have a life-raft pack (in a rigid container) if you are involved even in coastal cruising, you will often need to get ashore (to the pub, at least) when you are away from your own marina.

Where to stow the dinghy? If it is forward of the mast in a small sailing cruiser, it will foul the jib sheets. If it is aft of the mast on deck you will be for ever peering round it. Perhaps you will finally settle for towing the thing. See that the 'tow' is shortish and low down on the bow (outside) so that the dinghy rides bow up and doesn't fill, or affect the steering too radically. And see that it is secure. Chasing a dinghy is a time-consuming exercise and not particularly recreational.

Perhaps the best thing to do is to deflate the dinghy, roll it up and stow it. However, when you need it, it is a bore to pump the thing up. Half deflated, most dinghies will then stow best, bow forward, aft of the mast.

Your link with life

Incidentally, if that dinghy is your only means of survival in the event of a sudden sinking, don't stow the oars under everything in the 'sharp end' lockers of your craft. Oars made like tent poles (to fit together) and rowlocks should be very available to the dinghy, even lashed to it, especially if you are going on a long voyage. Also, if you have not got a proper life-raft, organize what might be called a survival bag, ready to hand. Cans of water, concentrated food, knife, compass, flares, sun lotion, etc. Work it out for yourself, and, if it does happen, try to get everybody to leave with plenty of clothing and a lifejacket.

Going ashore

A high percentage of the *comparatively* few fatalities in our sport occur whilst people are rowing or 'outboarding' between their craft and the shore. There we are, all dressed up to visit the local hostelry, with no thought of lifejackets (who wears one in a pub?). Everyone wants to go ashore together. Result, a heavily over-loaded dinghy with little between the sea level and the top of the side which, later at night, will be manned by the same lot who will have enjoyed themselves in a typically British way. Shrieks of laughter as we capsize or swamp and 'where's old Charlie?' Gone, on the ebb tide, and gone for good. This can, and should be, avoided.

Bilge pumps

Will our possible purchase ever start filling with water? If it does, can we get rid of said water?

Bilge pumps are designed to get rid of large quantities of water at high speed, should you ship huge green waves over the stern in bad weather.

Small leaks are always present and a once-weekly pump out will solve those. However, the day may come when you need a really adequate pump, easy to get at, easy to work with all your strength for perhaps several hours. Electrically operated ones save trouble until the electrics are swamped as well. I like to see one big bilge pump handy in the cockpit and another below decks. They should be checked constantly because matches are constantly being used and are often dropped; they are champion bilge-pump-jammers! The bilge pumps should have adequate filters and should clear the water through an outlet in the hull. Bilge pumps should not be an afterthought.

Toilets

Talking of pumps – let's take a look at the design of the 'heads'. Traditionally known by this name since the days of Nelson (when they were situated in the bows of the ship with no sophisticated pumping arrangements, except the bow wave as the ship dipped her nose into the next wave), 'heads' are a very important piece of ship's equipment.

The new types of re-circulating 'heads', which are emptied at disposal points, are becoming more standard in inland waters where craft are prohibited from using conventional equipment for environmental reasons. The traditional small-craft machinery at sea is a double action valve pumped by hand. The material is passed through a sieve in the side of the hull to disperse it and another pump operated to introduce sea-water as a flushing agent. Drop a cigarette or match down these and you have again jammed the pumps.

There are many different designs, and strangers on board should be instructed how to operate the machinery. It is always necessary to open a valve of some kind. Equally, it is important to instruct everybody to close the valve after use. Otherwise your ship could sink quietly by the 'heads'!

Self-draining cockpits

'Water, water everywhere, nor any drop to drink.' The design of even the smallest sailing craft should, wherever possible, include an arrangement for the day when the cockpit fills with water. That water *must* drain away by itself. In a sailing vessel, always heeled over one way or the other, there should be adequately sized drain holes at each corner of the cockpit floor. They should, of course, drain into the sea and not into the bilges.

For all this to happen, the cockpit floor obviously has to be above the level of the sea, so that gravity will assist the water to flow out. In very small craft this often presents a problem, because the cockpit becomes very 'shallow' and the crew get less protection from the weather. Lockers opening on to the cockpit and the 'companion way' to the cabin should all have permanent sills, for obvious reasons. To protect the crew, the considerate owner can erect canvas along the guard rails and stanchions adjacent to the cockpit.

Engines

I have already said something about maintenance, especially whilst laid up for the winter. Installation itself is a very big subject.

In the first place, a diesel engine is much safer than a petrol engine, but, for either, it is absolutely vital to see that the fuel tanks are adequately ventilated. Marine engines must have properly constructed vent pipes which cannot get blocked. Vapour from either diesel or petrol is more explosive than the fuel itself.

A petrol engine is much lighter than a diesel, horse power for horse power, so the chances are that a small sailing vessel will be equipped as standard with a petrol engine. It is also likely to have a smallish propeller to minimize 'drag' when actually sailing. You cannot therefore expect very high speed from a sailing vessel under power, nor very efficient rudder control.

In powered craft, the weight consideration is not so vital and I would opt for a diesel engine (or two!) every time. Diesels are less prone to trouble and are free from electrical ignition problems. However, to swing a diesel without mechanical assistance is well-nigh impossible, and, at best, tends to be a knuckle-barking exercise in a confined space.

Fuel lines and filters

Because of vibration, both petrol and diesel installations tend to suffer from fuel line problems. Engines in a marine and enclosed environment put one terribly at risk as soon as they develop anything approaching a leak of fuel.

I am told that there are 'plastic' lines which meet all necessary specifications. These are usually 'armoured', but I would always prefer to see good old copper with the odd coil in it to take up vibration.

I believe that you can never have too many filters and traps. 123

Anyway, you *must* have a filter between tank and carburettor in a petrol engine. It is superb for it to be transparent but, on the other hand, if it breaks, where are you? So, even if it is a little more trouble, let's have a metal 'cup' which, frankly, is not difficult to remove and inspect. On diesels, a glass filter 'cup' is less dangerous but you *must* carry spares.

Glass fibre fuel tanks

Glass fibre *can* be eaten by fuel. So again, see that tanks of this material at least meet the specifications laid down by an official body. The British Standards Institution does a fine job on many such items, and the Home Office lays down very strict rules about fire resistance.

Water cooling systems

I would also look carefully at the cooling system, especially on a second-hand boat. Fresh water circulates round the jacket of the engine itself and, somewhere during this circulation, it passes through the inner jacket of a 'heat exchanger' which transfers heat to the sea-water in the outer jacket. This has been pumped in and is circulating to 'collect' the heat and go out into the sea again. The inlet for this sea-water should be protected from the possibility of a plastic bag being sucked in, blocking the inlet, hence stopping the circulation of the sea-water with the obvious result of an overheating engine.

Another source of irritation, or danger, is the exhaust pipe. Where does it lead? Is it going to pass through a locker where you are keeping synthetic ropes or, worse still, fenders. If so, will it heat these up to the point where they weld into a glorious tangle of melted and solidified rubbish?

Stern glands

Of all the little bits and pieces tucked out of sight the stern gland is the one which causes most trouble. This is because the point where the propeller shaft passes through the hull is very vulnerable and you need to grease the bearings very regularly. There is also, of course, a lot of vibration, and, finally, it is out of sight, and out of reach to the majority of people, since, unfortunately, they do not possess the length of arm of a gorilla!

You therefore need a grease gun fixed in an accessible place, which has a pipe leading to the stern gland. You will need to give the gun a couple of screws downwards to force grease to the stern gland FAR more often than you think. Grease is cheap and boats are not. There is many a good boat lying at the bottom because some lazy Joe forgot to grease the stern gland. The shaft fractures – and makes quite the biggest aperture through which water can pass. If the gland even so much as leaks, in a heeled-over yacht, the sea-water can come in through the sump oil filler cap and quietly float the oil off all your bearings, ending in big-end trouble and big cheque trouble as well.

There is plenty which will never go wrong, and plenty which will sometimes go wrong, plenty also which will go right, but one thing is certain: the world of cruising boats is a world in which you never stop learning, and every winter evening could be spent reading yet another book on yet another specific subject all to do with the sport.

7. *Coast-wise*

Navigation

At the beginning of this book, I referred to the mumbo-jumbo of technical terms. There are many occasions when, to the uninitiated amateur seaman, the expert seems to be practising mumbo-jumbo.

My favourite example of this is the fellow who worked out at home from the tide tables that, during his cross-Channel passage, *the effect of the tides on the British side would be cancelled out by the French tidal movements*, if the vessel in which he was travelling maintained her usual average speed. He then only had to draw a line on the chart at home between his French destination and his port of departure and measure the course.

On board, he announced the course to steer.

Since he knew something which the others on board did not know, he came up on deck at about the time he expected to see the 'loom' of the lighthouse showing up on the clouds. This 'loom' is visible a long, long time before you can actually see the light of the lighthouse. Having spotted this faint glow, he sniffed the breezes, assessed the situation, contemplated his chart, accused the various people who had taken a turn at the wheel that they had not steered very exactly and advised a minor alteration in course. Hey Presto! The magic of the expert!

With practice and perhaps an evening institute course on navigation you, too, can be a master of the 'black art'.

Because of the change to metric measurements of depth on charts, the increasing number of Radio Beacons and new electronic navigational devices you may think that you need to be a metric conversion wizard, a master of the headphones and an electrical mechanic in order to be able to board anybody's vessel and say: 'I can navigate.' However, you can gain a basic knowledge of navigation very simply, and the tools you need for putting this into practice are remarkably few.

Their function and use are explained in the pages that follow – there really is no mystery about them.

Charts

First of all you need to buy a chart of the area in which you plan to sail. These charts are available from the Chart Agents listed below. Bear in mind, though, that any chart which you buy will need 'updating' or even renewing. There are continuously new things to put on your charts and these are announced by regular *Notices to Mariners*. You can get these posted to you by Chart Agents.

AGENTS FOR THE SALE OF ADMIRALTY
CHARTS AND HYDROGRAPHIC
PUBLICATIONS

British Isles

Aberdeen: Stevenson & Harris, 21 Regent Quay
Aberdeen: Berry & Mackay, 57 Marischal Street
Birmingham: see under Solihull
Blyth: Alder & Co., Ridley Street
Bristol: W. F. Price & Co., 24 Gloucester Road, Avonmouth
Brixham: Brixham Yacht Supplies, 72 Middle Street
Buckie: Thomas Garden, Harbour Office
Cardiff: T. J. Williams & Son, Ltd, 19 West Bute Street, Docks
Cardiff: Blair's Nautical Supplies, Ltd, 17 James Street, Docks
Chatham: Gransden Marine, 10 High Street
Chichester: Derry Long & Co., Ltd, 65 East Street
Chichester: Yacht & Sports Gear, 13 The Hornet
Christchurch: Purbrook Rossiter, Ltd, Bridge Wharf, Bridge
   Street
Cork: Cork Iron & Hardware Co., Ltd, 15–16 North Main Street
Cowes: Pascall, Atkey & Son, Ltd, 29 High Street
Dartmouth: Cobbold Marine, 5, 6, 7 Havley Road
Dover: Dover Marine Supplies, 166/7 Snargate Street
Dublin: Croxon & Dobbs, Ltd, 3 Windmill Lane, Sir John
   Rogerson's Quay, 2
Falmouth: Marine Instruments, 50 Arwenack Street, Hulls Lane
Folkestone: Folkestone Marine Ltd, Fishermarket, The Harbour
Glasgow: Kelvin Hughes, 123–145 North Street, C3
Glasgow: Christie & Wilson, 44 York Street, C2
Gosport: Hardway Marine Shop, Ltd, 95–99 Priory Road,
   Hardway
Greenock: Clyde Marine Motoring Co., Ltd, Prince's Pier
Grimsby: Olsens, Humber Bank, South, Fish Docks

Guernsey, C.I.: David Bowker, Pier Steps, St Peter Port
Holyhead: Holyhead Boatyard Ltd, Newry Beach
Hull: B. Cooke & Son, Ltd, 'Kingston Observatory', 58/59
    Market Place
Jersey, C.I.: W. H. Coom, South Pier Shipyard, St Helier
Leith: Thos. C. Lauder, 15 Bernard Street
Liverpool: Dubois Phillips & McCallum, Ltd, 8a Rumfort Place, 3
Liverpool: John Bruce & Sons, Ltd, Manchester Buildings,
    3 Tithebarn Street, 2
Liverpool: J. Sewill, Ltd, 36 Exchange Street, East, 2
Liverpool: J. Parkes & Son, 6, 8, 8a Windsor Street
London: J. D. Potter, Ltd, 145 Minories, EC3
London: Kelvin Hughes, St Clare House, Minories EC3
London: Lilley & Reynolds, Ltd, 9 Railway Place, Fenchurch
    Street, EC3
London: Capt. O. M. Watts, Ltd, 49 Albemarle Street, W1
London: H. Browne, Ltd, P. & O. Deck, P. & O. Building,
    Leadenhall Street
London: London Yacht Centre, 9 Devonshire Row, EC2
London: Brown & Perring, Ltd, 7 St Botolph Street, EC3
London: Boat Showrooms of London, Ltd, 288–290 Kensington
    High Street, W14
London: Thomas Foulkes, Lansdowne Road, Leytonstone, E11
Lowestoft: Kelvin Hughes, 2 Battery Green Road
Lymington: Peter Webster, Ltd, Ropewalk Boat Yard
Maidstone: Maidstone Marine, 27 Lower Boxley Road
Milford Haven: Blairs Nautical Supplies, Ltd, Victoria Road
Newhaven: Cantell & Son, Ltd, West Quay
Newport (Mon.): W. F. Price & Co., 111 Commercial Street
North Shields: John Lilley & Gillie, Ltd, Clive Street
Oban: W. Donnan & Son, Railway Pier
Plymouth: J. Blowey (Instruments) Ltd, Vauxhall Quay
Poole: H. Pipler & Son, Ltd, The Quay
Portsmouth: Gieves, Ltd, 2 The Hard
Ramsgate: Seagear (Ramsgate) Ltd, 54 Harbour Parade
Rye: Rye Marine Stores, Rock Channel
Sheerness: William Hurst, Ltd, 19 West Street
Solihull, Warwickshire: Hollywood Marine, Ltd, 123 Stratford
    Road, Shirley
Shoreham: A. O. Muggeridge, Ltd, Albion Street, Southwick
Southampton, SO1. 1BP: F. Smith & Son, Alexander House,
10/11 Queens Terrace

Swansea: Felix Martin, 2 Prospect Place
Teignmouth: N. V. Shannon, 8 Northumberland Place
Torquay: Geo. H. Wheaton & Sons, Ltd, 5 Beacon Quay
Ullapool: MacRae, Duggie, McPherson, Ltd, Shore Street
West Mersea: Clarke & Carter, Ltd, West Mersea
Whitby: The Whitehall Shipyard, Spital Bridge
Whitstable: Roy Rigden & Partners, Seawall
Woodbridge (Suffolk): Small Craft Deliveries, Ltd, 12 Quay Street

You also need to buy Chart 5011, which is not a chart at all. It is a description of all the symbols, marks and drawings which you will find on the charts proper. Having studied this, you will find that the charts themselves are quite easy to understand.

Buy a chart of your local area, the area you thought you knew so well. You will be fascinated to discover what it is really like and what goes on.

A compass or two

Compasses in small boats are magnetic compasses and operate by magnetic attraction to magnetic North. The attraction varies in different parts of the world and these variations are shown on the charts. Suppose, for example, you are in an area where the magnetic variation is 10° West. If you wanted to travel due North you would steer a compass course of 010 degrees; to travel East 100 degrees; South 190 degrees and West 280 degrees.

The compass will be fixed in the boat so that the 'lubber line' in the compass simulates the bow of the boat. If you read off the degrees against this lubber line you will know in which direction your boat is pointing.

You will also need a hand bearing compass. This is similar to the ship's compass and is useful because you can hold it in your hand and take a bearing on a particular object on land using a 'sight' on the prism, which allows you at the same time to read the bearing from the compass card.

I shall be discussing the advantages of being able to take a bearing of an object later on in this chapter.

The points of the compass

Whilst it is more usual nowadays to refer to angles and degrees, some mariners still use the points of the compass to indicate direction.

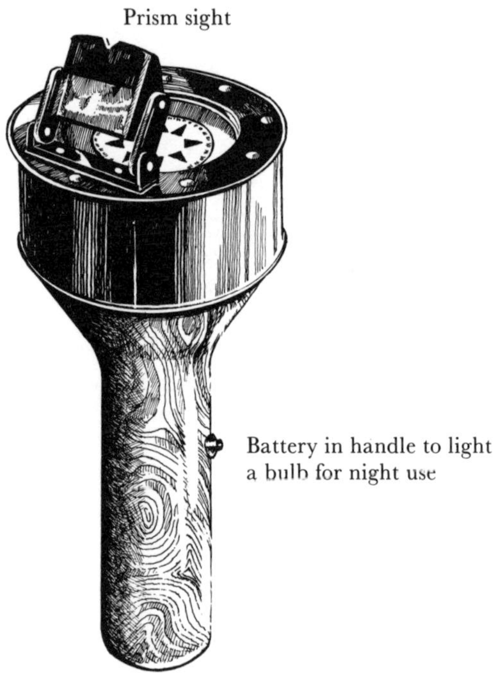

Fig. 62. A hand-bearing compass.

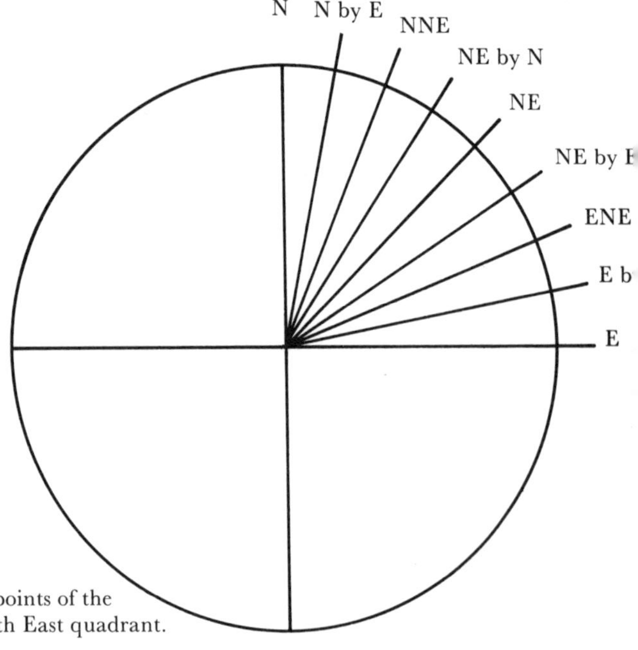

Fig. 63. The eight points of the
compass in the North East quadrant.

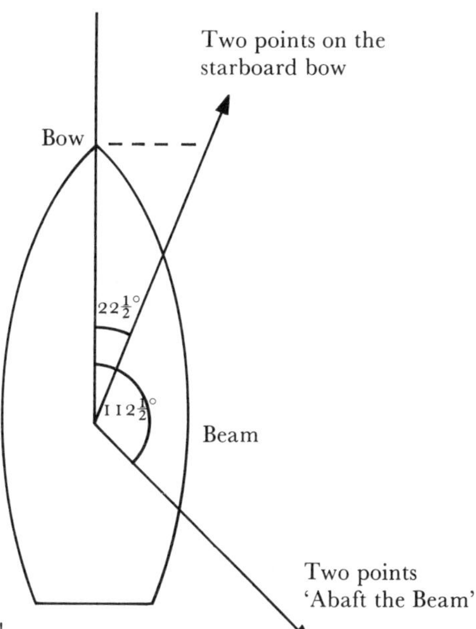

Fig. 64. Two points where?!

Bearing in mind that there are 360° in a circle, there are thirty-two points of the compass and therefore each is $11\frac{1}{4}$°. Thus, between North and West there are *eight* points of the compass. Fig. 63 shows the eight points in the North–East quadrant.

It follows that if somebody says 'two points on the starboard bow' you should look $22\frac{1}{2}$° from the bow of your vessel round to the right (Fig. 64). It also follows that 'two points abaft the beam' will be TEN points round the compass card, i.e. $112\frac{1}{2}$° (Fig. 64).

Some compass cards are marked off in both degrees and points of the compass.

A watch

You will, for many reasons, be lost without a good watch or ship's clock whilst at sea. You so often have to 'time' things, other than the boiled eggs! Particularly 'time elapsed', the 'period' of a light, or to be ready for weather forecasts at the correct time.

Your maritime 'milometer'

In a car you need a device to measure the distance you have travelled. It matters more in a vessel at sea. The apparatus can be of two sorts. The simplest sort is a 'patent log'. This is a long piece of special twine with a small rotator (propeller) at the end of it. 131

You 'stream' this behind your vessel and the rotator works a little dial rather like a couple of gas meter dials. The very latest sort of patent log is built into the hull and adds considerably to the expense of the boat. You do need one or the other because you must know, fairly accurately, how far you have gone.

Tide tables and tidal atlas

As I have already mentioned, up-to-date copies of tide tables and a tidal atlas should always be on board.

Echo sounder

Although an echo sounder is not an absolutely essential 'basic' instrument, you would be well advised to buy one. It indicates, if fitted expertly, the exact depth below the bottom of the boat, and helps to avoid running aground. However, it cannot 'see ahead'. It will only detect a gradual shallowing of the water. It will not spot a rock jutting up from the seabed a quarter of a mile ahead.

Before explaining how to use these few 'instruments' I should emphasize that there is little substitute for a proper course of navigation at either a nautical college or an evening institute. In a book of this scope I can only give you the bare bones of the knowledge you need to be able to navigate.

Taking bearings

Once you have plotted your course (allowing for tidal 'drift') and have set off along the coast, it is very necessary to keep track of where you are sailing. Having identified an object by reference to the chart, take a hand bearing compass and 'take a bearing'. Draw a line on the chart from the object at the angle which you read off on your hand bearing compass. It follows that you are somewhere along that line. Take bearings on two other identifiable objects (not too close to each other) and you should get a picture like Fig. 65. If your bearings are not quite accurate (because of yacht wobble) you will have a 'triangle of error' called by the black artists of navigation 'a cocked hat' (shades of Nelson!). Your vessel must, if you have done the job accurately, be somewhere in this triangle.

You may well think that if you can see all those things on the land, then you know where you are. To a certain extent that is

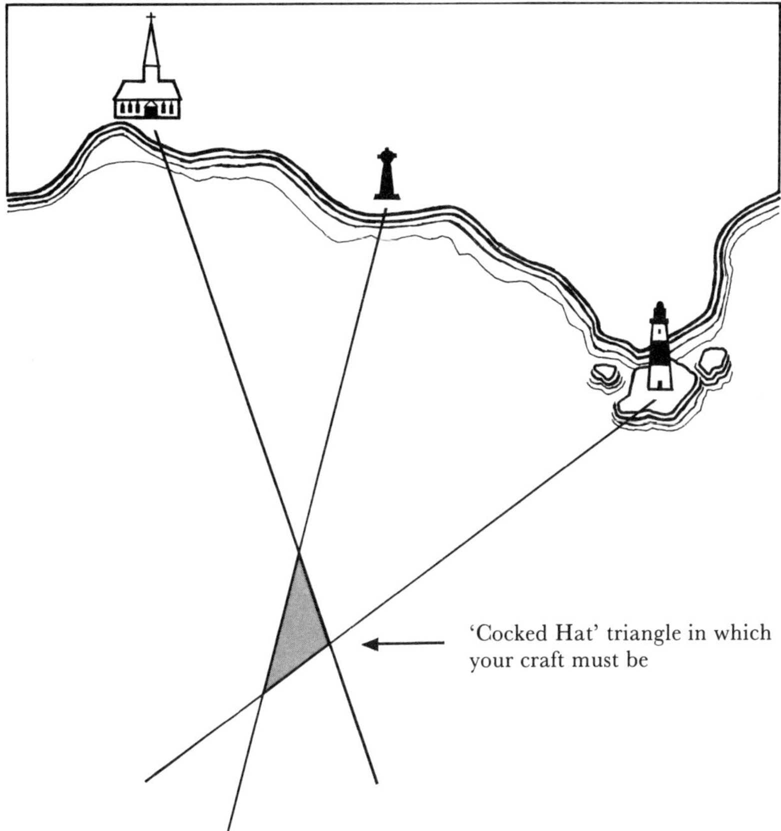

Fig. 65. Taking three bearings to fix
your position.

true, but it is a good thing to keep a check on your exact position. You may have miscalculated the tide or the time, etc., and realize that a radical alteration of plan or course is necessary.

Taking a running fix

Taking a 'running fix' is a useful method of fixing your position (or checking it) by taking a bearing on one object. In Fig. 66, take a bearing at A then time and take your distance to B, where you take another bearing of the same object. Then plot your work on the chart, having transferred your position line.

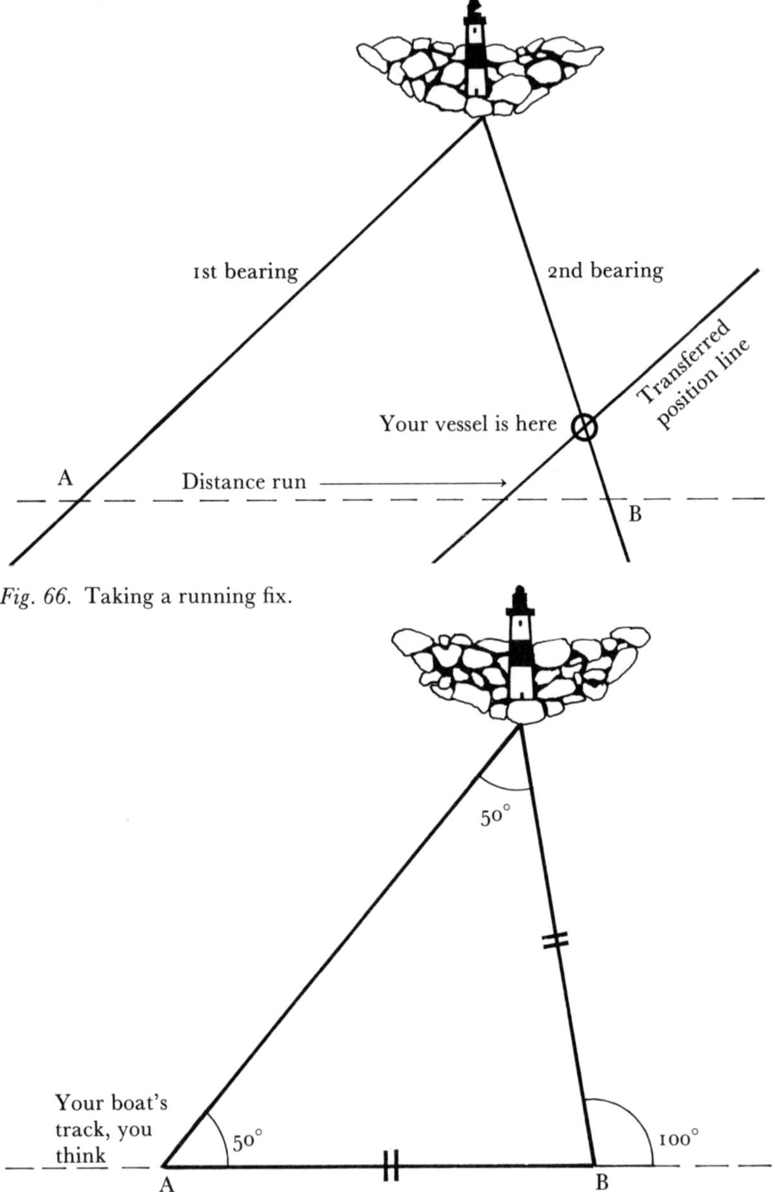

Fig. 66. Taking a running fix.

Fig. 67. Doubling the angle on the bow.

Doubling the angle on the bow

Another quick and reasonably simple method of finding distance off the coast is illustrated in Fig. 67. Basically it is inaccurate because you don't know whether the line AB is in fact the track of your boat. The essence of the idea is that you take a bearing of the object at A and measure your distance travelled until, exactly at point B, where the angle is doubled to the same object, you check the distance run and assume that the distance off the shore is the same as the distance which you have run, between the two points.

Those with an elementary knowledge of geometry will realize that they have plotted an isosceles triangle. The exterior angle equals the two interior and opposite angles; One interior angle you measured for yourself, then you waited until it was doubled! AND, if the two base angles of a triangle are equal then the sides opposite those angles must be equal. So, distance run equals distance off.

Transits

If you can manage to identify two objects on the chart which are dead in line, you know exactly where you are and whatever other exterior influences (such as the tide) may exist, you can be absolutely sure that you are 'on line'. The charts will show these transits at the approach to harbours, or you can find out about them from local pilotage books.

Clearly, if you line up two identifiable objects on the land you are bound to be 'on the line' drawn through them both on the chart.

Signposts of the sea

People who have never been to sea usually assume that lighthouses simply flash away at regular intervals. That is true, but no two are alike. Equally, buoys, which act as sort of intermediate lighthouses, are also quite distinctive and their characteristics are marked on the chart. The 'code' which they flash allows you to identify them. In a difficult area, like the Channel Islands, you may have in sight at the same time more than a dozen different characteristic lights which tell you where you are, since they are all marked on the chart.

During daylight, close in to the coast, you will also come upon many different coloured buoys, each of which tell you what to expect, where you are, and which course to take if making for a particular harbour.

Fig. 68. Buoys.

Buoys and buoyage systems

The British system (lateral) will eventually be changed to the Continental system (cardinal) which is *quite* different. However at present our system depends on the fact that all buoyed channels are marked from *seaward* as if you were floating in on the flood tide. At its simplest, on the RIGHT of the channel you will see conical buoys painted BLACK, and on the LEFT, can-shaped buoys painted RED. In very small rivers you may even see plain sticks on the RIGHT and plain sticks with an old rusty can perched on the top on the LEFT.

So, as in Fig. 68, you leave the RED cans to PORT and the BLACK cones to STARBOARD. Study the illustration carefully to ensure that you understand EXACTLY what I mean by *leave* the cans to port and the cones to starboard. You may reasonably find that the colours are not solid, but chequered patterns of red-and-white or black-and-white, but the *predominant* colour will be red or black, and their shape tells the rest.

To assist the big ship mariner there are also spherical buoys. These will have a *predominant* colour. If they are painted with *black*-and-white horizontal stripes you leave them to starboard. They denote, in fact, that you can go round them either side, but that the main channel is to their left. Equally, if they are *red* and white, in horizontal bands, you can go round either side but the *main* channel is to their right.

Wrecks are marked with green buoys, and usually have 'wreck' written on them. If these are can-shaped, leave them to port (same old rule!). If they are conical, leave them to starboard, and if they are round, go round them either side. Best of all, give them a wide berth. You can never be sure what hazard is below the surface.

To sum up: CANS to PORT, CONES to STARBOARD, ROUND ones which you go ROUND.

If you see any other shapes, look at the colour and treat them accordingly. If, for example, you see a round buoy which is red, black *and* white, in horizontal stripes treat it as an oddity, because it is! It is an isolated DANGER mark and should be given a wide berth as with a wreck buoy.

Lighthouses and lit buoys

The buoys which I have just mentioned may be lit at night. If they are, the cans may flash red lights or they may flash white *even* numbers, 2, 4 or 6. The conical buoys will flash *uneven* numbers, 1, 3 or 5 flashes and white lights.

There are many other distinctive signals that lighthouses or lit buoys give. They are all marked on the chart but, since the chart abbreviations may be a bit confusing, I set them out in full here, with their explanations. First of all there are *flashing* lights and *occulting* lights.

Flashing lights are designed so that the period of darkness is longer than the period of light.

Occulting lights are designed so that they are visible for a longer period than they are out. In fact, they are the opposite to a flashing light!

On the chart you will see the following letters and their meaning is as follows:

F.	Fixed. Steady and never goes out. There are few of these because they may be muddled with ship or shore lights.
Fl.	Flashing. Shows one single flash at regular intervals.

Qk. Fl.	Quick Flashing. Continuous flashing more than sixty times a minute.
Int. Qk. Fl.	Interrupted Quick Flashing. Flashes at more than sixty times a minute with darkness at regular intervals.
Gp. Fl.	Group Flashing. Two or more flashes in a group, at regular intervals.
Gp. Int. Qk. Fl.	Group Interrupted Quick Flashing. Groups of quick flashes with relatively long periods of darkness.
Occ.	Occulting. A steady light with a sudden 'darkness'.
Gp. Occ.	Group Occulting. Two or more sudden 'darknesses' in a group.
Alt.	Alternating. This is a light that changes colour whilst you are looking at it from the same place.

All these lights are not necessarily white. Many lights show in 'sectors' so that you may see a light green for a while and as you pass it, it may turn white and then red, or any variation of these.

Timing a light

An important point to remember is that the 'period' of a light is the gap between each series of flashes or whatever. A light flashing regularly is quite easy to time. If it is a group flashing light, the period is measured FROM THE START OF THE GROUP TO THE START OF THE NEXT GROUP. It is no good trying to identify a group by counting from the end of a group to the beginning of the next group. You will always be in a mess, wondering whether you are off Cherbourg or China!

Some people advocate having a stop-watch handy. Of course it helps, but can you see it in the dark? No! So you shine a torch on it and your last state is worse than your first. Having stared into a bright light, you look up and can see precisely damn all. Recognizing a light is either a group activity or one for which to be prepared. If you use a red filter on a torch, then your night vision is unaffected. Even your wife's red nail varnish can provide the all-important red filter. I have also found it quite useful to practise counting seconds. One – and – two – and – three – and – four – etc. It is remarkable how quickly you can train yourself to get it very accurate.

Running aground

Wherever you sail or power-boat, you are likely, sooner or later, to discover some 'ground covered by water' which you did not know was there, either because you have miscalculated the tides or because you have simply miscalculated the channel in a river or taken a headland a good deal too close. We can describe any of these eventualities, if we wish to be pompous, as 'errors of pilotage'!

I have said before that the level of the tide is more than important to you, and since there is a 'bar' (a ridge of built-up land) at the mouth of most rivers it is more than probable that, however careful you are, you will find yourself one day bumping on the bar, rather than leaning against one!

Because sailing boats tend to have deeper keels than power-boats, most of the advice that follows is directed towards sailing boat owners, but it will also be useful to those who have motor cruisers.

As soon as you feel your boat behaving oddly, shortening her pitching motion (fore-and-aft up-and-down motion) you can almost bet that the water is getting shallower. You will, if you linger, then get the odd 'bump' and you can be sure that you should alter course DRAMATICALLY for deeper waters. This, on hard and relatively flat surfaces, may be the end of your troubles, but on soft mud, especially in a sailing boat, you are likely to plough into it and stick.

On a falling tide, instant action is necessary and even on a rising tide there is no sense in lingering. It pays to 'get a move OFF!'

If under engine, go astern and, in a sailing boat send the crew forward. Their combined weight will depress the bow, and might free the deepest part of the keel which is, normally, towards the stern of the boat. If under sail with no engine, as soon as you bump, go about smartly. If you do stick try to turn the boat's head towards deep water. Back the jib, forcibly, Clearly, however, if running downwind you cannot do that so you must drop your sails at once because they are only driving you further on to the ground.

If you are on a rising tide there is less need to 'panic' and if you cannot get off, row away in the dinghy with the kedge anchor and lay it in a sensible place to enable you to pull the boat off as the tide rises. Fig. 69 gives an idea of one set of circumstances where the kedge anchor will probably do the job.

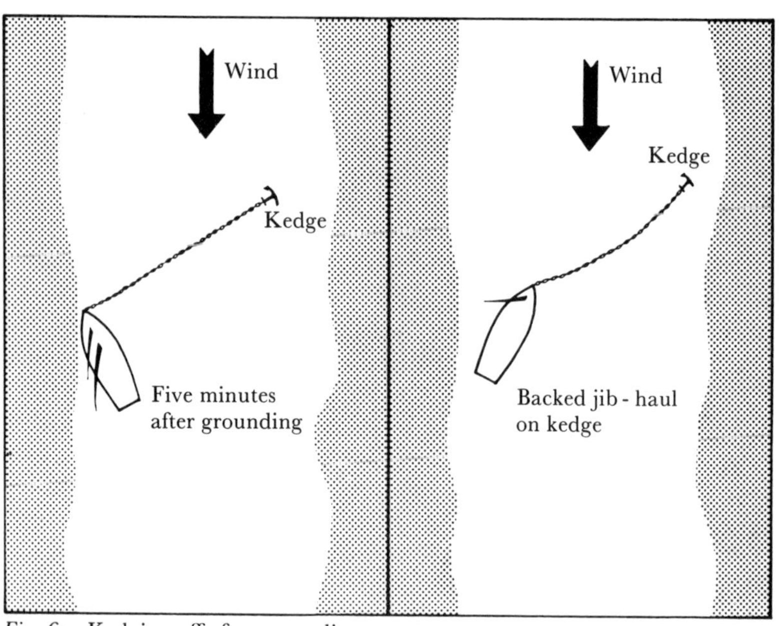

Fig. 69. Kedging off after grounding.

Fig. 70. Keep away from a lee shore even if you *are* on the wrong side of the channel.

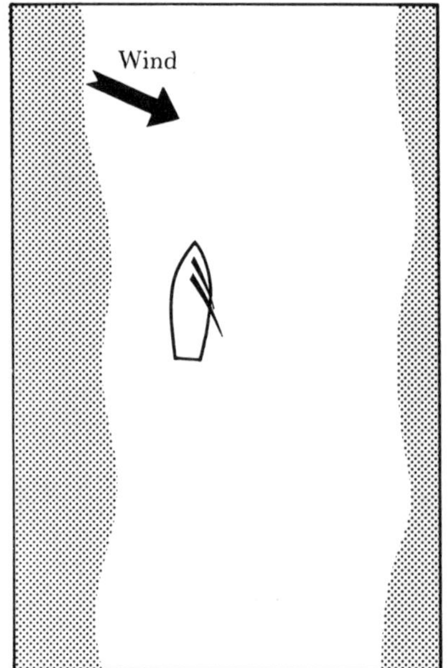

As you will realize, a lee shore, which I explained earlier, is the worst place to touch. Therefore, always sail your boat, wherever possible, a safe distance from a lee shore, even if it means that you are not adhering to the elementary cry of 'keep to the right of the channel' (see Fig. 70).

Lastly, please appreciate that if you do run aground at the top end of the highest spring tide, the next tide may not reach your boat for almost a fortnight. Actually it is true to say that if you must run aground it is best to do it in the morning, because the afternoon tides *tend* to rise a little bit higher. Frankly, the best advice of all, is don't risk running aground. Do it by mistake once, especially in an exposed position, and you will for ever after remember the appalling way in which the mast 'twanged' every time she bumped!

Heavy weather

It seems sad to end a book about the pleasures of using your own boat to 'get away from it all' with a section on how to deal with the situation should the weather worsen whilst you are at sea, but it is a vital piece of knowledge. If you can help yourself, others will not have to venture forth, perhaps risking their own lives to sort you out. Just to bring you back to the technical terms for a moment – you can reef, heave-to, lie ahull, or run before the storm.

Reefing

Sailing vessels can reduce their sail area by reefing, motor cruisers, being faster, can make all speed to the nearest shelter. Even dropping an anchor on the 'quiet' side of a headland will suffice.

Sailing boats take longer to get there, but those with an engine should consider the same sort of action. If the assessment is, however, that the weather will worsen too quickly for you to gain shelter, you are safer out at sea, reefing once you have got there and changing down headsails to their smallest.

Heaving-to

The next action, having found plenty of sea room (i.e. being *well* away from a lee shore) is to 'strap' the jib the wrong side ('back the jib'), adjust your reefed mainsail and lash the tiller or wheel in a position which leaves the boat virtually stationary in the water. 141

You will then move very slowly at right angles to the wind, drifting a bit to leeward.

Lying ahull

Not much to be recommended, because it means that you take off all sail, lash the tiller or wheel to leeward so that the boat lies beam on to the wind and sea. You will roll around but should be safe. What the rolling motion will do to the well-being of your crew is, however, nobody's business. Incidentally if they *are* going to be sick try to explain that it is better over the side *not* facing the wind!

Running before the storm

This, in my opinion, is the safest way of coping with bad weather. Remembering that the average cruising chap is not forced to go to sea, nor forced to return to the harbour from whence he came, I would take off all sail except the very smallest jib and steer, not *dead* downwind, but to one side or the other of the wind direction, as far as possible keeping your stern to the waves.

The problem will be the LARGE waves which appear to be chasing you, and the awful feeling that they are going to break over the stern. To help them break before they reach you, stream every available rope you have behind you. If you have a long mooring warp, tie one end to the starboard quarter and one to the port quarter and let it out in a great loop behind you. The effect will be to slow down your boat (a good thing) and also to help those waves to break on the rope rather than on your stern. If you happen to have any quantity of oil on board it is a great agent for 'smoothing troubled waters' and will tend to be carried along in the loop of rope which you put out.

The end of the voyage

When you have returned to port, put the boat away and climbed into your car for the journey home, I hope you will be able to say 'everything I did was as good as it could be'. I am always very conscious that anything I do could be bettered. Boating is as rewarding as any sport I know, and I hope that, despite the dire warnings contained in this book, you are not put off trying to gain the experience necessary *not* to frighten yourself, your family, or those who are concerned with rescuing the foolhardy from their follies. Know your own capabilities, leave a little in reserve, both of strength and knowledge, and you will enjoy it all immensely.

Amateur Swimming Association,
Harold Fern House,
Derby Square,
Loughborough, LE11 0AL
Leics.

Association of Pleasure Craft Operators,
26 Chaseview Road,
Alrewas,
Burton-on-Trent,
Staffs DE13 7EL

Beach Rescue Advisory Committee,
Rosebank,
Ringmore,
Shaldon,
Teignmouth,
S. Devon.

British Canoe Union,
70 Brompton Road,
London,
SW3 1DT

British Canoe Union Coaching Scheme,
c/o 70 Brompton Road,
London,
SW3 1DT.

British Sub-Aqua Club,
70 Brompton Road,
London,
SW3 1HA.

British Water Ski Federation,
70 Brompton Road,
London,
144 SW3 1EG.

British Waterways Board,
Craft Licensing Supervisor,
Willow Grange,
Church Road,
Watford, WD1 3QA
Herts.

English School Swimming Association,
190 Nether Street,
London,
N3.

Inland Waterways Association,
114 Regents Park Road,
London,
NW1 8UQ.

Lloyd's Register of Shipping,
Yacht and Small Craft Department,
Lloyd's Register House,
69 Oxford Street,
Southampton,
SO1 1DL

National Coastal Rescue Training Centre,
Afan Lido,
Aberavon,
Port Talbot,
Wales.

National Federation of Sailing Schools,
Christian Sailing Centre Ltd.,
Dodnor Creek,
Newport,
Isle of Wight.

National Federation of Sea Anglers,
7 Hayes Hill Road,
Hayes,
Bromley,
Kent,
BR2 7HH.

National School Sailing Association,
Richard Aldworth School,
Western Way,
Basingstoke,
Hants.

Offshore Powerboat Club of Great Britain,
5 Hereford Court,
Worcester Road,
Sutton,
Surrey.

Royal Life Saving Society,
Desborough House,
14 Devonshire Street,
Portland Place,
London,
W1N 2AT.

Royal National Life-boat Institution,
West Quay Road,
Poole,
Dorset.

Royal Ocean Racing Club,
20 St James's Place,
London,
SW1A 1NN.

Royal Society for the Prevention of Accidents,
Royal Oak Centre,
Brighton Road,
Purley, Surrey,
CR2 2UR.

Royal Yachting Association,
Victoria Way,
Woking,
Surrey,
GU21 1EQ

Scout Association,
25 Buckingham Palace Road,
London,
SW1W 0PY.

Ship & Boat Builders National Federation,
31 Great Queen Street,
Kingsway,
London,
WC2B 5AD.

Sports Council,
70 Brompton Road,
London,
SW3 1EX.

Surf Life-Saving Association of Great Britain,
4 Cathedral Yard,
Exeter,
EX1 1HJ.

Swimming Teachers' Association,
National Headquarters,
1 Birmingham Road,
West Bromwich,
Staffs.

Yacht Brokers, Designers & Surveyors' Association,
Orchard Hill,
Farnham Lane,
Haslemere,
Surrey.

Yacht Charter Association,
33 Highfield Road,
Lymington,
Hants.

Appendix 2. Glossary

ABACK	When the wind presses on the wrong side of the sail.
ABAFT	Nearer the stern than something else.
ABATE	When the wind force lessens, it is said to abate.
ABEAM	At right angles to the fore-and-aft line.
ABOARD	On board a ship.
ABOUT	When a vessel passes her bows through the wind, she 'goes about'.
ACCOMMODATION	Sleeping and domestic space aboard.
ADRIFT	Anything loose, unfastened or missing is said to be adrift.
AFT	Towards the stern, behind.
AGROUND	When the keel of a vessel rests on the bottom of the sea.
AHEAD	In front of the vessel.
AHULL	A vessel lies ahull when, in bad weather, it drops all sail to ride out a storm.
ALOFT	Above the deck.
AMIDSHIPS	The middle of the ship or, of helm, dead centre.
ANEMOMETER	A device for measuring wind strength.
ANCHOR	The act of dropping anchor. A 'hook' to hold the ship.
ANSWER	Of a vessel, when she changes direction following alteration of the rudder, she 'answers her helm'.
ASTERN	Behind; in the direction of the stern.
ANTIFOULING	Paint for the underwater surface of a vessel, to prevent marine growth.
ATHWART	Across the vessel's width.
AWASH	Just under or washed over by water.
BACK	A sail is 'aback' when the wind is on the wrong side of it. The wind 'backs' when it changes direction anti-clockwise.
BACKSPLICE	Used to prevent a rope unravelling.
BACKSTAY	A wire rope from masthead to stern, to prevent mast falling forward.

BAGGY-WRINKLE	Padding on stays or shrouds to prevent chafe of sails.
BAILER	Any small receptacle used to remove water from a boat.
BALLAST	Weight carried in or on a vessel to counter-balance top weight or wind pressure on sails.
BAR	A shoal or shallow area formed across the mouth of a river by the action of tide or current.
BATTEN	A flexible piece of wood, metal or plastic placed in a pocket on the leech of a sail to prevent curl or flap.
BATTEN POCKET	Slot to accommodate batten in sail.
BEAM	The extreme width of a vessel.
BEAM REACH	Sailing with the wind at right angles to the fore-and-aft line.
BEAR AWAY	To alter course away from the wind or another vessel.
BEAR OFF	To push away any object, move away from a quay.
BEARING	The compass direction in which an object lies from you or your vessel.
BEAT	A vessel beats to windward, when close hauled and having to tack.
BECALMED	When there is no wind, a vessel is 'becalmed'.
BELAY	To make fast a rope to any object, particularly a cleat; an order to cease any activity.
BEND	To put a sail on its spars or to fasten one rope to another.
BEND	A form of knot used to attach a rope to a bar, spar or ring.
BERMUDIAN (BERMUDAN)	Fore-and-aft rig without gaff or yard.
BERTH	A sleeping place on board or a place to dock a vessel, i.e. an alongside berth.
BIGHT	A loop in a rope.
BILGE	The curve of the bottom of a ship and the space beneath her cabin 'floor'.
BILGE KEEL	A fin on the side of the bottom of a boat to provide stability.
BINNACLE	The construction in which the ship's compass is fixed.

BITTER END	The last piece of any rope or chain.
BITTS	Posts, rather than cleats, to which chain or mooring and towing ropes may be attached.
BLOCK	A pulley through which any rope passes over a grooved wheel.
BOBSTAY	A wire or chain to restrain the upward pull of a bowsprit.
BOLLARD	A post, drum shaped, usually on shore, to which warps or mooring lines are fixed.
BOLT ROPE	A rope sewn along the edge of a sail.
BOOM	The horizontal spar to which the foot of sail is fixed.
BOOM-CRUTCH	A fitting to support the boom end in harbour.
BOOT-TOP	The joining line between bottom and topside paint.
BOSUN'S CHAIR	A seat, usually wooden supported by rope, for use when being hauled aloft to inspect or repair mast or rigging.
BOTTLE SCREW	A double-action screw for tensioning rigging.
BOWER	The main anchor.
BOWS	The forward end of any ship.
BOWSE	To pull down or tension any rope, i.e. bowse taut.
BOWSPRIT	A spar, forward of the bow, to which a fore-sail stay may be fixed.
BRAIL	A rope or strip of material to furl and spill wind from the mainsail.
BREAKER	The crest of a wave which is breaking.
BREAST ROPE	A mooring line from bow or stern to the nearest point on the quay.
BRIDLE	A length of rope fastened at both ends and controlled from the middle.
BRING UP	To anchor, or stop.
BROACH-TO	When running before the wind to sheer off in either direction despite the helmsman's efforts.
BULKHEAD	Any partition dividing the interior space of a vessel athwartships.
BULWARKS	A solid construction, similar to guard rails, to stop crew falling overboard (pronounced 'bullocks').

BUMPKIN	A 'bowsprit' at the stern to which a backstay is attached (pronounced 'bumkin').
BUNK	A 'bed' on board.
BUNKBOARD	Of wood or canvas, to prevent a person from falling out of his bunk when the yacht is heeled over.
BUNT	The middle part of a sail.
BUNTING	The material used for making flags or (slang) the flags themselves.
BUOYANCY	An airtight construction on any craft (or person) to give support in the water.
BURGEE	A triangular flag flown at masthead denoting club or organization.
'BY THE LEE'	Running before the wind with wind on the same side as the boom. Not recommended.
CABLE	Approximately 200 yd distance, or chain connecting anchor to craft.
CAN BUOY	A flat-topped buoy usually indicating port side of channel.
CANOE STERN	An overhanging stern with pointed end.
CARRY AWAY	When rigging or gear, of any kind, breaks, it is said to carry away.
CARVEL	A method of boat construction using flush planking.
CAST OFF	To let go.
CAVITATION	Vibration caused by incorrect size or position of propeller.
CENTRE-BOARD	A hinged or sliding movable keel slid through the bottom of a boat to provide lateral resistance. Otherwise, known as a centre-plate.
CHAFE	To rub or wear.
CHAIN PLATE	The metal permanent lower end fixing of any standing rigging.
CHART DATUM	The level from which all depths are measured on a chart.
CHARTER	To let or hire a vessel. The hirer and the document of hire are known as the Charter-party.
CHINE	The angle where topside of hull joins the bottom in certain designs of craft.
CHRONOMETER	An accurate clock used for navigation.

CLEAT	A wood or metal fitting, T-shaped, to which a rope is secured.
CLEW	The lower after corner of a triangular sail.
CLINKER	A method of boat construction using overlapping planking.
CLOSE-HAULED	When a craft is sailing as near to the wind as possible, she is said to be 'close-hauled'.
CLOSE, TO	When any two objects are apparently coming into line or when a vessel comes near to another or to the shore, each is said to be 'closing'.
COACH ROOF	A raised portion of deck to allow headroom below.
COAMING	Any vertical construction on deck protecting hatches, cockpits, etc., from the ingress of water.
CONSTANT BEARING	The angle between two vessels. If this is not altered or does not alter there is a risk of collision.
COCKPIT	The 'well' in which crew and helmsman sit or work when not 'on deck'.
CODLINE	Small line used for lacings, etc.
COMPANIONWAY	The entry from deck or cockpit to accommodation.
COMPASS POINT	A division on the compass card. There are thirty-two compass points; each measures $11\frac{1}{4}°$.
COUNTER	Of boats, an overhanging stern.
COURSE	The direction in which a craft is steered.
COURTESY ENSIGN	When entering a foreign port, the maritime flag of that country is worn.
CRINGLE	A metal reinforced hole in a sail.
CROSSTREES	Struts fitted to mast to spread shrouds for greater strength and 'staying' power.
CROWN	The 'head' of an anchor.
CUDDY	A small covered-in fore-deck forming a cabin of sorts.
CUTTER	Single masted fore-and-aft rigged vessel with two headsails, usually with a bowsprit.
DAGGER BOARD	Unpivoted centre-plate. Vertical plate used in small dinghies.

DAN BUOY	A weighted buoyant marker buoy.
DAVITS	'Cranes' for hoisting small boats aboard larger ones.
DEAD-EYE	Any D-shaped or circular fitting through which any rope may be secured.
DEAD RECKONING	The plotting of a craft's position by distance run, and course steered. Properly 'deduced' reckoning (D.R.).
DECK HEAD	The under surface of the deck.
DECK LIGHT	Any 'skylight' let flush into the deck.
DECK LOG	Notes of all alterations of course, speed and time, etc., for future dead reckoning plot.
DEVIATION	Any error of magnetic compass caused by the yacht's magnetism.
DIP	To lower and re-hoist the ensign by way of salute to other vessels.
DISPLACEMENT	The actual weight of a vessel, or the water it 'displaces', which is equivalent.
DODGERS	Canvas screens on the guard rails to protect cockpit.
DOGHOUSE	A protective construction built over a companionway.
DOGWATCH	Two two-hour watches of duty between 4 p.m. and 6 p.m. and 6 p.m. and 8 p.m.
DOWNHAUL	Any tackle or rope used to restrain a spar or sail from upward movement.
DOWN HELM	To push the helm to leeward to bring the vessel towards the wind.
DRAG	Used of anchors when they are not holding the craft.
DRAW	When the wind fills the sail it is said to 'draw'. A craft also 'draws' so many feet of water, i.e. the depth from waterline to bottom of keel.
DRESS OVERALL	To hoist the international code flags and wear from stem to stern over the masthead, on festival and special occasions.
DRIFT	Without motive power, to move with tide or wind.
DROP KEEL	See Centre-board.
EASE	To slacken a rope.

EBB	The receding tide.
ECHO SOUNDER	An electronic device which by the emission of a sound and the measurement of its 'return' indicates the depth under the keel.
EDDY	Circular motion of water not associated with mainstream.
EIGHT BELLS	Each half-hour of a four-hour watch is marked by the ringing of a bell. Thus halfway through the watch is four bells.
ENSIGN	The national flag (maritime or otherwise) worn to denote a vessel's nationality. The red, white or blue ensign is used in British ships. Not the Union flag.
FAIRLEAD	An 'eye' or other fitting through which a rope is passed to alter its direction or keep it free of obstruction.
FAIRWAY	The navigable part of a channel.
FATHOM	Six feet.
FENDER	Any object used to prevent damage to a vessel's topsides in harbour or elsewhere.
FEND OFF	To push clear.
FETCH	To reach a destination without having to tack.
FIDDLE	Any vertical construction on tables, lockers, etc., to restrain objects from sliding off or out.
FIT OUT	To prepare a vessel for a voyage or for a new season.
FIX	A check of position derived from plotting position lines having taken bearings or other accurate observations.
FLAKE DOWN	To coil down a length of rope so that it will run out without tangling.
FLOTSAM	Goods lost overboard by mistake (see Jetsam).
FLY	The horizontal length of a flag, the other being the hoist.
FOOT	The lower edge of a sail.
FORE-PEAK	In a yacht, the space immediately in the bow, below decks.
FOR'ARD	The opposite of aft (i.e. Go for'ard).

FRAP	To secure ropes to increase their tension. Yacht halyards are said to be 'frapped' when secured away from the mast. Very important in Marinas!
FREER (or freeing wind)	A wind moving further abeam tending to allow the easing of sheets.
FULL AND BY	Sailing close-hauled on the wind direction rather than maintaining compass course.
GAFF	An upper spar to which the head of a sail is bent.
GAFF JAWS	The mast-end fitting upon which the gaff slides.
GAFF SAIL	A quadrilateral sail for use with a gaff.
GALLEY	The 'kitchen' on board any craft.
GENOA	A large triangular foresail usually extending abaft the shrouds.
GIMBALS	A fitting which allows anything to remain level even when the craft is heeled. (The compass, galley stove and lamps are usually gimballed.)
GOOSENECK	The fitting attaching boom to mast.
GOOSEWINGED	A vessel running before the wind with sail set on both sides is 'goosewinged'.
GUDGEON	A metal circular fitting attached to the stern into which the rudder pintle fits.
GUNTER-RIG	A vessel with triangular mainsail with part of the luff attached to a vertical spar.
GUNWALE	The uppermost edge of a vessel's side.
GUY	A wire or rope attached to a spar to hold it in position.
GYBE	To bring the wind through the stern (when running) so that the boom swings to the opposite side.
HALYARD	A rope or wire used for hoisting a sail or flag.
HAMBRO LINE	Small diameter rope for lashings or lacings.
HANK	A clip to hold the luff of a sail to a stay.
HANK ON	The act of clipping the luff to a stay.
HARD	A permanently constructed landing place.
HARDEN IN	To sheet in. To haul in sheets.
HARD DOWN	To put the helm fully to leeward.

HATCH	Any opening in the deck which has a cover, sliding or hinged.
HAWSE PIPE	A hole below the gunwale through which the anchor cable runs.
HEAD	The bow of a vessel. The top of a sail.
HEADBOARD	A strengthened piece of sail at the head. On larger vessels the strengthening may be of wood or metal.
HEADROOM	Below decks height from sole to deckhead.
HEADSAIL	A sail set forward of the mast.
HEADWAY	The forward motion of a vessel through the water.
HEAD WIND	A wind from dead ahead.
HEADED	A close-hauled vessel is said to be headed when the wind shifts, necessitating alteration of course.
HEAVE-TO	To back the jib and adjust the mainsail to 'hold' the vessel from forward motion.
HEAVING LINE	Light rope, usually weighted, used to pass a heavier rope to another vessel or the quay.
HEEL	To lie over or list.
HELM	The tiller or wheel, NEVER the helmsman.
HELMSMAN	One who manipulates the tiller or wheel.
HITCH	Used to make a rope fast to any object. A quick tack.
HOIST	To haul up. Also the name of the vertical edge of a flag or sail.
HORSE	A bar athwartships upon which the mainsheet block travels.
HOUNDS	Where the lower rigging is attached to the mast.
HOUSE FLAG	The private flag of an owner, shipping line, company or association.
HULL	The whole of a craft to deck level.
IRONS, IN	A sailing craft is said to be 'in irons' when she will not pay off on to either tack.
JETSAM	Goods deliberately thrown overboard (see Flotsam).
JIB	The foremost headsail.

JUMPER | A stay passing over a spreader forward of the mast.

JURY RIG | Any temporary rig, erected following breakage of the craft's conventional rig or as a makeshift form of propulsion.

KEDGE | A light anchor generally used with rope; the main anchor being the bower anchor (preferably equipped with chain).

KEEL | The fore-and-aft basic structure of the hull.

KICKING STRAP | A rope or tackle (never a strap) to restrain the boom from lifting.

KING PLANK | The centre plank of a planked deck.

KNOT | The joining of ropes. A measure of speed – one nautical mile (6,067 ft) per hour.

LACING | Any small line to fasten sails, dodgers, etc.

LANYARD | A short rope to connect rigging to hull, or secure some small object (knife, whistle) to any object.

LASH | To bind or secure with rope.

LATITUDE | Distance in degrees either side of the Equator (e.g. 35° N.).

LAY UP | The act of taking a craft out of commission. To bring ashore for winter.

LAZARETTE | A small locker right forward or aft.

LEAD | (Pronounced 'led'.) A weight on a measured line used for measuring depth of water (taking soundings).

LEE BOWING | Sailing a boat so that the tide is on the lee bow, thereby pushing the boat up to windward. This tends to increase speed.

LEECH | The after edge of a sail.

LEE HELM | If the design of a craft is such that she tends to bear away from the wind, she is said to 'carry lee helm'.

LEESIDE | The side of a craft furthest from the wind.

LEE SHORE | A shore on to which the wind is blowing.

LEEWAY | The sideways movement of a craft.

LIFELINE | Often used to describe a line passing through stanchions, otherwise known as a guard rail. Alternatively a line rigged centrally fore and aft in heavy weather.

L.O.A.	Length overall. The extreme length of a vessel.
LOCKER	A cupboard of any kind on board.
LOG	A book (log book) containing a record of craft's movements. Otherwise a device for measuring distance run (a 'patent' log).
LONGITUDE	Distance in degrees either side of Greenwich meridian (e.g. 14° E.).
LOOM	Part of an oar inboard of the rowlock. The glow of a light reflected on the clouds.
LUBBER LINE	The mark on the compass bowl in line with the vessel's head.
LUFF	The forward edge of a sail. A vessel turning closer into the wind is said to luff.
L.W.L.	Load water line. The (imaginary) line on the hull at which the vessel floats when laden to her designed weight. In yachts this is often referred to as waterline length.
MAIN (sail)	In a fore-and-aft rigged craft, the sail aft of the mast.
MAKE FAST	To secure (or belay) any rope.
MAKE SAIL	To set the sails or increase sail area.
MARLIN-SPIKE	A pointed instrument for opening strands of rope or the pins on shackles.
MARE'S TAILS	White 'feathered' clouds indicating an increase in wind force.
MAST STEP	The 'footing' into which a mast is placed either on deck or on the keel.
MEAN	A prefix indicating average, i.e. mean level.
MERIDIAN	A true north-and-south line.
MISS STAYS, TO	When the helmsman fails to bring the craft about on to her new tack and she falls back on to the original one, the craft is said to 'miss stays'.
MIZZEN (mast)	The after mast of a yawl or ketch. In larger sailing ships, the after mast of a vessel with more than two masts.
MOOR	To tie (moor) a vessel to a quay or posts or between two anchors.

NAVEL PIPE	The hole and pipe down which the anchor chain passes to the chain locker.
NEAP TIDES	Tides between full and new moon with a lesser range than spring tides.
NEAPED	A vessel aground is neaped when the next tide will not refloat her.
NIP	A sharp bend causing wear in a rope where it passes through a block, sheave or fairlead.
OFFING	Distance off the shore.
OFF THE WIND	Any attitude of sailing except 'close-hauled'.
ON THE WIND	Close-hauled.
OPENING	Of transits; as the vessel leaves the exact line the marks appear to be 'opening'.
OUTHAUL	Any gear used for stretching a sail along its spar.
PAINTER	The rope attached to the bow of a dinghy by which she may be secured.
PALM	A fitted leather pad used by a sailmaker.
PATENT LOG	An instrument for measuring distance run.
PAY OFF	When a vessel's head falls away to leeward she is said to 'pay off'.
PAY OUT	Of line or rope, when it is slackened or lengthened.
PENNANT	Any pointed flag other than a burgee.
POOP	A vessel is said to be 'pooped' when an overtaking sea breaks over her stern.
PORT	An object is on the portside when it is to the left, looking forward towards the vessel's bows. Also used of a round 'window' in a vessel's side.
PORT TACK	A sailing vessel is on the port tack when the wind is blowing on to her left side (looking forward over the bows).
POSITION LINE	A plotted line, derived from a bearing, which determines the likely position of a vessel.
PRAM	A dinghy with a blunt bow and stern, i.e. with a transom at both ends.
PURCHASE	A system of rope and blocks used to increase the power of a given effort. Hence 'block and tackle' (pronounced 'take-al').

QUARTER	The after-part of the side of a vessel.
RANGE	The difference between the highest and lowest level of any tide: the distance a power-driven vessel can travel on its fuel capacity.
REACH	A sailing vessel 'reaches' when the wind is crossing the boat approximately at right angles.
REEF	To reduce the area of sail.
REEVE	To pass a rope through a fairlead, block or dead-eye.
RIDING LIGHT	Otherwise known as an anchor light. A white all-round light in the forepart of the vessel.
RIGGING SCREW	See Bottle Screw.
ROACH	The outward curve of the leech of a sail.
ROUND UP	To turn the vessel's head up into the wind (to facilitate the hoisting of sails).
ROWLOCK	A U-shape into which an oar fits when rowing (pronounced 'rol-lock').
RUDDER STOCK	That part of the rudder closest to the stern post.
RUN	To sail before the wind.
RUNNER	A movable stay to support the mast.
RUNNING RIGGING	Any movable sheet, halyard or rope used to control sails (as opposed to fixed stays and shrouds to support the mast, known as standing rigging).
SAMSON POST	Any strong post designed for securing anchor chain or towing lines to it.
SCOPE	The length of chain between anchor and vessel.
SCULL	To propel a boat by working one oar used over the stern.
SCUPPER	A hole in the bulwarks to allow shipped water to drain away off the deck.
SEA ANCHOR	An open-ended conical canvas bag which is 'towed' to reduce speed (e.g. in bad weather).
SEACOCK	A valve, in any pipe which exits through the hull, to prevent sea-water 'back-flowing'.
SEAM	The stitching on a sail or the space between two planks.

SEIZING	A binding.
SERVE	To bind, for protection against chafe, with thin line.
SHACKLE	A U-shaped piece of metal with its open mouth closed by a bar, usually with a screw thread.
SHACKLE KEY	A special tool for unscrewing a shackle bar.
SHAKE OUT	To free a reef from a sail.
SHANK	Part of an anchor joining arms to ring.
SHEAVE	The grooved wheel in a block over which a rope runs.
SHEER	The convex curve of a vessel's shape in the vertical plane. A concave curve is known as a reverse sheer.
SHEER	To alter the position of a vessel relative to her anchor by applying helm.
SHEET	A rope used to trim a sail, i.e. to alter its angle relative to the wind.
SHEET-IN	The act of trimming a sail.
SHIP	To bring or receive on board, especially 'to ship a sea' when waves come over the deck.
SHROUD	A wire rope to support a mast athwartships – fore-and-aft supports are called stays.
SLACK WATER	The 'pause' between ebb and flow of tide when there is no tidal stream.
SLICK	Any smooth patch of water especially that caused by a vessel's hull, if driven sideways by windforce.
SNUB	Used of a vessel, at anchor, snatching at the cable. To arrest movement of rope or cable.
SOLE	The cabin floor.
SOUND	To take measurement of depth beneath a vessel's hull.
SOUNDING	The measurement of depth of water.
SPINNAKER	A full-bellied triangular sail set on the opposite side to the mainsail when reaching or running.
SPITFIRE JIB	A very small foresail used in heavy weather.
SPLICE	The interlacing of strands of a rope or ropes to form a join.

SPREADERS	Otherwise crosstrees – lateral spars fixed to the mast to spread the rigging for greater support of the upper portion of the mast.
SPRING	A mooring line to restrain a vessel from moving forwards or backwards.
SPRUNG	A cracked mast or spar is said to be 'sprung'.
STANDING PART	The main part of a rope especially that part which is made fast and not hauled upon.
STARBOARD	The right-hand side of a vessel when looking forward towards the bows.
STARBOARD TACK	A sailing vessel is on the starboard tack when the wind is blowing on to her right side (looking forward towards the bows).
STAY	A wire rope giving fore-and-aft support to a mast.
STEERAGE WAY	A vessel has steerage way when moving sufficiently fast through the water to answer her helm.
STEM	The main timber in the vertical plane at the bow of a wooden vessel. Used also to denote the bow of a vessel constructed in material other than wood.
STERN BOARD	When a vessel 'in irons' moves fast enough astern to answer her helm she is said to 'make a sternboard'.
STERNPOST	The aftermost part of a vessel to which the rudder is attached.
STOPPER KNOT	A knot made up on a rope to prevent it from unreeving or to hold it in place temporarily or permanently.
STOPS	A sail is 'in stops' or 'stopped' if it is gathered and bound with easily broken twine (stopping cotton) so that it may be set and broken out when needed.
STRUM BOX	A strainer on the end of the suction pipe of a bilge pump.
SWIG	To tighten a rope by alternating the pull round a cleat and a pull on the standing part.
TABERNACLE	A fitting on deck into which the heel of a mast, capable of being lowered, is fitted and pivoted.

TACK	The lower forward corner of a fore-and-aft sail: a point of sailing.
TACK	To beat to windward along a zig-zag path.
TACK TACKLE	A purchase applied to the luff of a fore-and-aft sail to stretch the luff taut. A down haul at the forward end of the boom on a Bermudian rigged vessel (pronounced 'tack take-al').
TACKLE	A combination of various blocks (pulleys) and associated rope to increase the efficiency of effort (pronounced 'take-al').
TAFFRAIL	The rail round the stern. In modern yachts often referred to as the pushpit.
TAIL	A short rope spliced to a wire rope, or one attached temporarily.
TANG	Any metal fitting on a mast or spar to which rigging may be attached.
TENDER	A yacht is said to be tender when she heels too easily: a dinghy belonging to a yacht.
THIMBLE	A pear-shaped grooved ring of metal round which a rope may be permanently spliced to protect it from chafe.
THWART	A seat across the centre of a dinghy. Sometimes used of any flat 'seat' in a dinghy.
TIER	A strip of canvas used for securing a mainsail to the boom when stowed (pronounced 'tie-er').
TILLER	A bar protruding forward from the rudder which the helmsman uses as a lever to turn the rudder.
TOPPING LIFT	A rope (uphaul) to support the boom-end when the sail is not completely set.
TOPSIDES	The outside of the hull between water and deck level.
TRANSOM	The flat stern of a dinghy or other vessel.
TRYSAIL	A heavy canvas small mainsail set in heavy weather in place of the vessel's usual mainsail.
TUMBLE-HOME	The inward curve of a vessel's hull above the waterline. Some yachts have a pronounced convex curve from gunwale to waterline.

TURN UP	To belay, or make fast, a rope on a cleat or belaying pin.
UNBEND	To remove a sail from its spar.
UNDER WAY	A vessel neither at anchor, nor made fast to the shore, nor aground.
UNION 'JACK'	Only correctly used when the Union Flag (surrounded by a white border) is hoisted in the bows.
UNSHIP	To remove anything from its appointed place.
UP HELM	To put the helm to windward, so that the vessel bears away.
VEER	To pay out anchor cable. The wind 'veers' when it changes its direction in a clockwise direction.
WAKE	The path which a vessel leaves in water astern of her.
WARP	Any rope to make a vessel fast or to haul it from one position to another.
WEAR	Strictly an *ensign* is worn, a *flag* is flown.
WEAR SHIP	To change tack by passing the vessel's stern through the wind (i.e. gybing). Outdated term really applicable to square-rigged vessels.
WEATHER	A vessel 'weathers a mark' if able to pass to windward without tacking.
WEIGH	The act of raising the anchor.
WEND	To turn a vessel about, passing bows through the wind. (Outdated)
WHIP	To bind twine round the end of a rope to prevent it unlaying (unravelling).
WINCH	Any drum-shaped rotating mechanical appliance on to which a rope may be turned to provide increased effort to haul in.
WINDLASS	A form of winch especially used for anchor chain.

| YARD | A spar on to which a square sail or topsail is bent. |
| YAW | To fail to keep a steady course. To swing from side to side. |

A PRACTICAL

1. HANDLING OF BOATS UNDER OARS

pulling	thole pins	removing rowlocks
oars	sculling notch/rowlock	stowing oars
rowlocks	coming alongside	making boat fast
crutches	after use	

2. HANDLING SAILING BOATS ASHORE

types of trolleys and trailers	care in support
economy of effort	securing to trolley

3. HOW TO SELECT AND MAKE SAIL ACCORDING TO CONDITIONS, INCLUDING REEFING

mainsails	roller reefing
working jibs	reef points
reefing principles	furling
when to reef	cleating of halyards

4. SAILING A COURSE (solo-conditions permitting)

a. Getting under way from beach, hard and mooring
b. Picking up moorings, beaching, coming alongside
c. Knowledge of points of sailing and basic manoeuvres
d. Knowledge of the basic and simple Rules of the Road

5. RIGHTING A CAPSIZED DINGHY

stay with boat –	jib sheets
get immediate control	'Scooping up' crew*
disposition of crew members	Help helmsman aboard
leverage on centre plate	bail out
aids to climbing aboard –	plug centre-plate box

(*Note:* * This method is known to all RYA instructors and forms part of the RYA teaching method.)

Capsize drill is a practical requirement of the Elementary Certificate. No certificate may be issued without this requirement having been fulfilled, though the Log Book may be marked up to show completion of the certificate training except for this item. Principals of establishments may, however, decide to postpone (not cancel) this requirement in conditions where it would be dangerous to undertake the drill.

B THEORY (onshore teaching)

1. BASIC KNOWLEDGE OF BOAT PARTS AND THEIR USES

centre-board (plate)	mast step	leech of sail
dagger-board	halyard	luff of sail
rudder	shrouds	foot of sail
pintle and gudgeon	fore stay	tack of sail
tiller	boom	clew of sail
mainsail	mainsheet	roach of sail
foresail/jib	jib sheet	shackle
mast/heel/truck	head of sail	jib hank

2. PRACTICAL ABILITY TO TIE BENDS AND HITCHES

Figure of eight knot	Bowline
Reef knot	Fisherman's bend
Sheet bend	Clovehitch
Double sheet bend	Round turn and two half hitches

3. RECOVERY OF MAN OVERBOARD

Methods:

in over side	single handed sailing
practice	aids to climbing aboard
keep man in sight	

4. SAFETY AFLOAT IN RESPECT OF PERSONAL AND BOAT BUOYANCY

buoyancy aids   built-in boat buoyancy
lifejackets   solid boat buoyancy
BSS 3595 ('69)   buoyancy bags
when to wear   buoyancy checks/repairs
types of lifejacket   fixing of buoyancy
disposition of buoyancy –
too much, too little

5. ELEMENTARY FIRST AID AND LIFESAVING

likely accidents   effects of sea water on wounds
mouth to mouth resuscitation   sea sickness
first aid kit   exposure

6. DISTRESS AND SAFETY SIGNALS

Types
Flares, types and use of
Flags or shapes?

7. WINDS, TIDES AND CURRENTS AND THEIR EFFECT ON SAILING DINGHIES

tidal sequence
tide tables and tidal stream atlas
ebb and flow
visible indications of tide
wind effect on high and low water
spring and neap tides
speed of boats relative to sailing with a current and against
wind and tide together
wind against tide
shallow water effects

8. RULE OF THE ROAD

Knowledge of the steering and sailing rules

 C TIDAL

1. **SAILED A GIVEN COURSE ON TIDAL WATERS**

Accompanied by an instructor in the vicinity of moored boats
and other obstructions. To include: launching, getting away;
all points of sailing: tacking, gybing, coming ashore or alongside.

British Canoe Union Sea Proficiency Test for a Kayak

SEA PROFICIENCY TEST (kayak only)

(*Note:* The purpose of this test is to ensure that the candidate has sufficient knowledge and skill to enable him to take his kayak safely to sea **under a competent leader**.)

The test must be taken at sea, under moderate conditions. Allowance will be made by the examiners if conditions are rough, but the kayak skills must be performed in a competent manner. For reasons of safety, three kayaks will participate. The test will not be taken in a flat calm.

The candidate will:

1. Present himself suitably equipped for the test.

2. Present for inspection the following items, which must be both suitable and serviceable:
   a. kayak, paddle and spray cover;
   b. bow and stern toggles and/or safety lines and/or painters;
   c. buoyancy;
   d. lifejacket;
   e. repair kit and simple first aid kit;
   f. rudder and steering gear if fitted. (It is recommended that the kayak be fitted with rudder and steering gear);
   g. waterproof kitbag(s).

3. Pack his waterproof kitbag(s) with the necessary items for a day tour and stow it (them) in the kayak. In addition to those items listed at 2 above, the following should be included:
   a. spare clothing;
   b. packed lunch;
   c. equipment for providing a hot drink;
   d. emergency food;
   e. flares;
   f. whistle;
   g. torch;
   h. matches (or lighter);
   i. polythene bag of minimum size 6 ft × 3 ft for use in exposure cases.

4. Demonstrate:
a. launching and embarking. He will paddle at least 50 metres off shore into deep water – i.e. well out of his depth;
b. efficient paddling technique, forwards and backwards;
c. turning the kayak 360 degrees in both directions by using sweep strokes. If the kayak is fitted with a rudder, he will, whilst paddling evenly on both sides, turn his kayak again in both directions, this time steering with the rudder only;
d. emergency stops, forwards and backwards;
e. drawing the kayak sideways in both directions;
f. slap support;
g. paddle brace high and low on his left and right;
h. stern rudder.

5. Demonstrate:
a. bringing the kayak alongside a jetty or another kayak;
b. bringing the kayak into a beach forwards, sideways and backwards. (If the kayak is fitted with a rudder, the candidate will not be required to bring the kayak to the beach sideways or backwards.)

6. Perform capsize drill, followed by a deep water rescue with his partners. He will take charge of a rescue and then act as a capsized patient.

7. Prove that he can swim. He will then swim 50 metres in canoeing clothing (wet or dry suits are permitted) and a fully inflated lifejacket.

8. Answer questions on:
a. his practical experience, giving firm evidence of his having taken part in at least three one-day expeditions at sea;
b. safety precautions applying particularly to the kayak at sea;
c. the general effects of tide, current and wind;
d. local coastguard organization and rescue services;
e. local waters and conditions.

9. Show that he can do simple tidal predictions by the tidal constant method.

Index

173